1982

Oriental Children
in
American Homes

Oriental
Children
in
American
Homes

FRANCES M. KOH

East-West Press
P.O. Box 4315, Minneapolis, Minnesota 55414

To Edith B. McCrea

Acknowledgement

I wish to give special thanks to families (parents and children) and their teachers who graciously shared their experiences with me and contributed much material for this book. Although I wish to mention them each by name, I'm unable to do so since I promised to preserve their privacy. However, when they read this book they will know where they made their contributions.

Carol Liesmaki read the entire manuscript and offered helpful comments and suggestions. I thank her for her assistance and encouragement. My thanks also go to Grace Sandness and Ann Merriam for their editorial assistance.

My greatest debt is to "sister," Edith B. McCrea, without whose support and understanding this book would not have been written. To her, it is dedicated with affection.

Contents

Introduction

This book is intended primarily for the general public, especially adoptive families, as well as others interested in either comparative culture or American adoption of Oriental children. It interrelates two large fields—culture and cross-cultural adoption. However, a word of caution is useful here. Since each field covers a large, complex area, this book in these pages cannot discuss in depth many aspects of each. Rather, the writer attempts to discuss from a certain focal point only *some* aspects of each field that directly relate to the experiences of adoptive families.

The adoption of Asian children by American couples began sometime after the conclusion of World War II, as some concerned Americans responded to the plight of children fathered by American servicemen in Japan, during the American occupation, then in Korea, during and after the Korean war, and more recently in Vietnam. Inevitably, American presence in these countries resulted in a number of children whose fathers are American. However, people in these countries are highly homogeneous and put a strong emphasis on "pure-blood" lineage. As a result, children of mixed parentage are not only unaccepted into the mainstream of their society, but are often subjected to mistreatment, even persecution by their schoolmates and others. This makes it very difficult for their mothers to raise and care for them. Moreover, when these children grow up, they have little chance for the successful adult life accorded to other children in their country.

According to Helen Miller, in her article, "Recent Developments in Korean Services for Children" in *Children Today*, American adoption of Korean-born children began in 1953, when the Seventh Day Adventist church placed a few children with American families.[1] This was soon followed by Harry Holt's adoption program, which placed mixed-race children in American, Canadian and Western European homes. In subsequent years, as their programs expanded, the Holt Adoption Program began to place war orphans and abandoned children as well. The success of the Holt's overseas programs has given rise to a number of social agencies in Korea, which are active today in similar programs.

Meanwhile, in the United States during the 1960's and 1970's, because of the wide-spread use of contraceptives, the availability of legalized abortions, and society's increasing tolerance toward unmarried mothers raising their own children, the number of children available for adoption has been drastically reduced. As a result, social workers have sought new sources of adoptable children and found one in displaced Asian children (in Korea,

Hong Kong, Vietnam, etc.).[2]

As these historical factors in both continents merged, hundreds of displaced Asian children found their way to American homes. Many of these children were older than four or five at the time of placement, and some were much older. When adoption takes place across racial and cultural boundaries, there are many adjustments to be made by the families involved. Whether the child is from Korea, China, Japan or Vietnam, he comes with the stamps of Confucian culture and upbringing. He comes with a set of habits and attitudes already formed in that culture. The majority of the children do not speak a word of English. One 19-year-old girl who came here at age 11 said, "I didn't understand American culture. My parents didn't understand why I was doing things in certain ways. Whatever I did, I did in my Korean way, but it was the wrong way. I was really confused and couldn't understand what they expected from me. When they told me something, I couldn't explain or respond to them, due to the language barrier. It was so frustrating!" On the other hand, parents experienced equal frustration due to cultural barriers. One exceptionally sensitive mother who adopted an 8-year-old girl said, "Our experience hasn't been just childhood problems. We had culture shock! For months, I was completely in the dark . . . felt absolutely alone. I was so hungry for some insights into the behavior of our child. Most of the reports we read or hear about are glowing—but I know there is the dark side. How can we talk more openly and honestly?" Some parents can see and feel more than others. Likewise, some children present more problems than others. Regardless, culture shock is an inevitable result of cross-cultural adoption, and it has to be met with understanding.

Cultural differences in East Asia and America are enormous, as the essence of Oriental culture is based on Confucianism and Buddhism, while that of American culture is based on Christianity and Individualism in the tradition of John Stuart Mill. Each culture is truly the antithesis of the other in many ways. For this reason, when American parents and a Confucian child are brought together in a family situation, they are bound to have some culture-related problems, as well as other kinds. No matter how old he is, culturally speaking (in terms of American culture) the child's life begins at zero in his American home. It is my firm belief that a successful adjustment for the child is highly dependent on his understanding of his new environment as well as his parent's understanding of the culture in which he was reared. This mutual understanding is crucial to the development of their relationship. But I believe the parents must assume the greater responsibility.

Experts in the adoption field advise that prior to the arrival of their child, the parents learn something about the culture and customs of the country of the child's origin. However, most American parents enter their adoption with little knowledge of Korean culture, let alone an understanding of its cultural effects on the child. This is not entirely their fault. Social agencies must assume the greater part of that responsibility. While there are few published materials available about Korean culture, there are almost none that relate Korean culture to the cross-cultural experiences of adoptive families or vice versa.

In the early 1970's, when I was involved with a parents' support group, I came in contact with many parents who adopted Korean-born children. We spent much time talking together and learning from each other. Often they expressed the need for a book that could relate Korean culture to their experiences. I also saw the need and was interested in writing such a book, but at the same time I realized that to do so would take an enormous amount of time, energy and funds. I also faced the problem of finding enough families with certain backgrounds to interview. Finally, in 1976, I began to write a book which compares American and Confucian cultures, the subject which had interested me for many years.

Then, in 1978, through the cooperation and encouragement of one family of my acquaintance, I had the opportunity to interview a sizable number of families, who contributed much of the research material to the writing of this book. This book is a synthesis of my work on culture and adoption. Part of the research material also comes from my earlier contacts with various families whom I met, talked with, and counseled on various occasions. In all, I have had contact with more than sixty persons (parents, children and teachers). Most of them were quite willing to be interviewed, some of them were even enthusiastic to cooperate, and most were generous in sharing their experiences with me. However, one mother in charge of a project for a parents' support group refused to be interviewed on the ground: "We have enough facilities here to help adoptive families. We don't need a book!" For some families, my interviews served as catharsis for releasing their deeply buried frustrations that had no access to release. I promised the families I interviewed that whatever experiences they shared with me would be confidential. Thus, I am obliged to protect their privacy; for this reason the names I have used in this book are fictional.

The experiences I quoted in this book are those of

families who adopted a child or children from four to 16 years of age at the time of placement. My assumption is that by three or four the child has already internalized some basic patterns of response to the external world, conditioned by the way he was treated by his parents and others during his first few years of life.

Therefore, when he is placed in an American home, the child has to make some adjustments. The older the child the more adjustments he must make. Regardless of age, however, the success of the child's adjustments will largely depend on the attitudes and resourcefulness of his parents—most importantly, their understanding of his needs, needs determined by his past as well as his present environment.

With this in mind, I decided to cover some of the most basic and important areas directly related to the experiences of adoptive families, in which the American parent and Confucian child are most different in their cultural orientations. For instance, what kind of adjustments must the child make in his eating and sleeping habits? These are relatively simple areas of adjustments; more complex adjustments must be made in the psychological, social and linguistic areas. The older the child, the greater the challenge. How can parents help the child overcome his trauma of separation or cope with the stress which results from change of culture? How does the child who had never been kissed or hugged respond to his American parents' kissing or hugging? How does the child who had learned only Confucian relationships of inequality adjust to American relationships of equality? How does the child who had been oriented to dependency from his infancy adjust to American orientation of independence? Do the parents find the American way of discipline effective with the child? What aspects of the child's basic personality did the parents find most difficult to cope with in terms of their own? What kind of errors did the child most frequently make in learning to read or speak English, and why? How was the child's general performance in school, as well as his motivation to learn? How did the parents and teachers handle name-calling the child encountered in school or in the street? These are some of the questions I have attempted to answer.

This book also discusses the motivations of couples to adopt, reactions of their relatives, friends or public, as well as their own expectations and rewards. The motivations to adopt a child vary among couples. The largest group of parents in this study did not have children because of infertility, late marriage or being single, but wanted to create a family. The next largest groups already had a child or children born to them or adopted, but wanted to give their child a sibling of the same sex. The third largest group had either boys or girls and wanted the experience of parenting children of the other sex. A few appeared to be motivated by the need to satisfy their "rescue fantasy." In addition, the book discusses parental attitudes and views on the quest for the child's identity. Do they see the child as American, as Korean, as an individual human being with various backgrounds, or as a combination of all these? Which aspect is more important? Different parents have different answers.

Most problems adoptive families have had to cope with seem to me to be directly or indirectly culture-related. Therefore, a family's ability to cope with these problems depends on its understanding of the relationship between the culture in which the child was brought up, his thought processes and actions. Psychiatrist Abram

Kardiner writes in *The Psychological Frontiers of Society*, "The concept of culture with the aid of psychodynamics can become a powerful weapon of interpretation."[3] Indeed, to be able to interpret a particular problem accurately, one must be thoroughly familiar with the concepts of culture and psychodynamics, as well as be able to relate the two areas as they apply to a particular family problem. In addition, it is helpful to have had the first-hand experience of living with people of both cultures. This background of mine has been a great help in writing this book —in developing the ideas and selecting the areas discussed, as well as the research methods or approaches used.

Research methods or approaches greatly depend on the purpose of the research. This book is not intended to develop any theory or theories, or to draw any conclusions about the subject matter discussed here. The primary purpose is to describe the qualitative differences between Confucian and American cultures, in the light of the concept of culture and psychodynamics, as well as how the cultural differences are reflected in the experiences of adoptive families. Thus I set out to find out what kinds of problems families encountered in certain areas, in an attempt to provide some insight into problems each family experienced.

To be sure, each family has its own unique experiences to relate, yet I see a common thread running through the experiences of many families I've met and talked with. I believe each family will find something it can recognize and identify with in the experiences of the families presented in this book.

1
Physical
Adjustments

Food

Food, like other basic components of his childhood, can affect a person throughout his life. A man may move into another, totally different culture and may change his general value-attitudes in the matter of a few years as a result of acculturation, but he does not easily give up his preference for the foods on which he grew up. This has been the case with most Korean-born children who have been adopted by American couples.

Since American and Korean foods are considerably different from one another in kind and in methods of preparation, these children may find American foods to be one of their biggest adjustments. So it is advisable that parents learn about their child's food habits before his arrival.

The diet of Koreans, Japanese or Chinese, is high in starch and low in protein and fat, in contrast to the

American diet which is high in protein and fat. Basic ingredients of the Korean diet are rice, fish, vegetables, soy food, seaweed, noodles, potatoes, along with occasional chicken or beef. Since meat and dairy products are scarce and expensive, protein is supplemented mainly by fish and soy food.

Traditionally, infants are breast-fed. In cases where maternal milk is not available or sufficient, substitute foods such as goat's milk, grated apple or gruel are used.[1] Gruel is made of rice or beans finely ground with a pebble against the ribbed surface of a serrated mixing bowl. Today dried milk is available in the market, and some city dwellers use it for their infants. However, the use of milk for infants is still very much limited to a small segment of the urban population.

Some parents reported that their Korean-born children developed milk or other food allergies or indigestion, after they were introduced to American foods. This was probably due to the type of fat and protein contained in the milk, cheese, and baby foods to which those children were not accustomed. One 16-year-old girl who came here at age 11 said, "In the beginning I had a hard time getting used to milk and cheese. I kept throwing up. So my mom gave me American foods slowly, to get me used to them."

Thus, it is advisable that children, especially infants, be introduced quite gradually to American fat- and protein-rich foods, and that they be given only moderate amounts of milk, in addition to rice or bean gruel, oatmeal, and the grated apple mentioned earlier.

Unlike the American custom, in Korea there is no great difference in the kind of foods served at breakfast, lunch and supper. The basic foods served at each meal are rice, *kimch'i** (pickled cabbage), soy food of some kind and vegetables, augmented by a choice of fish or meat. Some poor people eat almost nothing except rice, *kimch'i* and fish. For table utensils families use chopsticks and spoons made of either brass, silver or wood, depending on their financial means. Meat or vegetables are chopped or sliced into small pieces, so as to be easily picked up with chopsticks.

Among all Korean foods, rice and *kimch'i* are the most essential daily foods; a meal is indeed inconceivable without either. Rice is served with *kimch'i,* along with other side dishes. At meals each member of the family has his own rice or soup bowl; all other dishes are placed in the center of the table and shared with others. An adoptive mother reported that their newly arrived 8-year-old child tried to keep for herself the big bowl of rice which had been prepared for the entire family. The child probably thought the bowl was for herself alone, since in Korea she had always been given her own bowl of rice at each meal.

Learning that rice is the staple of Korea, many adoptive parents stock a large quantity of it before or with the arrival of their child. One mother said, "We bought a 25 pound bag of rice and the whole family began eating rice and *kochoo'jang* (hot pepper paste). Most of my family like it, but I can't eat really hot foods." *Kochoo'jang* is made of finely ground chili peppers, flour (wheat and soybean), honey or other ingredients. In fact, *kochoo'jang* is as important to Koreans as ketchup is to Americans. It is used as seasoning for various dishes, including vegetables and soups.

---

*Korean words are romanized (spelled in English alphabet) in several different ways. The McCune-Reishauer system is used in this book.

Next to rice, the most important food in the Korean meal is *kimch'i* (pickled cabbage). *Kimch'i* is served at each meal. It can be made from a variety of seasonal vegetables such as cabbage, cucumbers, and white radishes. Most commonly, however, it is made of celery cabbage (so-called Chinese cabbage). In the fall, almost every family buys large quantities of this cabbage and makes a winter's supply of so-called winter *kimch'i*. The cabbages are stored for fermentation in large, earthenware crocks, usually placed on a concrete platform near the kitchen. In the northern cities where winter temperatures fall below zero, the crocks are often buried in the ground and covered over with straw to keep them from freezing. Present-day apartment dwellers, equipped with refrigerators, leave the dressed cabbage at room temperature for a day or two, until it becomes sufficiently fermented, then refrigerate it to keep it from becoming sour. It should be noted, however, that *kimch'i* is prepared in many different ways from a variety of ingredients, depending on the taste and skill of the maker. In the old days (still true in most parts of the country) the important test for a housewife was her skill at cooking rice and making *kimch'i*.

Almost all Koreans gorge themselves on *kimch'i*. It has a pungent smell, due to the garlic used in its making and the fermentation of the cabbage. It tastes invariably hot and often sour. Its sourness resembles the taste of sauerkraut and dill pickles. As a result, many children will favor dill pickles and sauerkraut. One mother who adopted two girls said the girls "love" sauerkraut and pickles. However, some parents may find the strong smell and sharp taste of *kimch'i* disagreeable. One mother said, "The girls are very proud of us because we like *kimch'i*." Stories about *kimch'i* are numerous among families. One mother who adopted a 5-year-old boy said, "He has an enormous craving for *kimch'i*. Whenever we take him to a Korean restaurant, he gobbles up several dishes of it at once." A teenage girl raised celery cabbages in her family's backyard to make *kimch'i* and invariably initiated her friends to it. A mother who adopted a 12-year-old girl said, "Soon after she came, we went on a camping trip. We took a jar of *kimch'i* as a special treat for Susan. In the morning my husband and I went fishing on the lake. At one point, when I turned around, I saw Susan eating *kimch'i*. I was just horrified that she would eat it the first thing in the morning, instead of cornflakes with milk. I scolded her, 'You don't eat *kimch'i* for breakfast.' She was hurt and disappointed. Then, later on, I learned that in Korea she always ate *kimch'i* at breakfast." Another mother who adopted two teenage boys said, "I made *kimch'i* before they came. It was terrible . . . but they ate it. They didn't mind it. I didn't realize how important *kimch'i* was and how they missed it when they didn't have it. Since their Korean mother came to the United States, she provides the boys with *kimch'i* via parcel post."

On the other hand, some parents reported that their children who have been here for some time can no longer eat *kimch'i* as hot as they used to. A mother said, "We eat *kimch'i* from time to time, but, unfortunately, our boys can't eat it as 'hot' as they once did." A 17-year-old adoptee reportedly cannot eat *kimch'i* now without rinsing it with water.

Next to rice and *kimch'i*, soup is a very important food, especially at breakfast, and consumed in large quantities daily. Soups are usually made of soybean paste and water mixed together, to which are added vegetables such as spinach, bean sprouts, scallions or cubes of soybean curd. Others are commonly made of water and soy sauce, with cod or beef and vegetables.

As already discussed, the major sources of protein in the Korean and Japanese diets are fish and soybean products. Of all soybean products, soy sauce is the most important item, as it is used in preparing almost all dishes. The next item widely used is soybean paste, which is used mainly in making soup. Soybean curd, probably the richest in protein, is used in preparing all kinds of dishes.

Traditionally, almost all families make their own soy sauce and soybean paste, because they are used a great deal every day and because the process of making them is fairly easy. However, this is not the case with soybean curd. In season, families buy large quantities of soybeans, which they soak in water and cook in a large caldron all day, until they are thoroughly soft. Then the steaming beans are pounded with a large, wooden mallet in a stone or wooden mortar until they become a soft mass. Out of this mass are made many, small, pyramid-shaped heaps. These heaps are dried in the sun or at room temperature until they become hard, then are dumped into large, glazed, earthenware crocks of salt water for fermentation. After a while the salt water becomes dark brown, which means it is ready to be used as soy sauce. The soybean heaps are taken out of the crocks, mashed, and put in other crocks to be used as soybean paste.

Fish and shellfish, the other major sources of protein, are abundant in the seas around the peninsula. There are many varieties, such as sardines, cod, shrimp, oysters, haddock, crab, squid, octopus and scallops. Usually, families who live on the coast buy large quantities of fish in season, particularly cod, haddock and squid, then salt and dry them for use all year. Dried fish is often used as a snack with rice wine.

Seaweed (laver and kelp) is also consumed in great quantities by Koreans and Japanese, because it is considered rich in minerals and vitamins. Dried laver comes in about 7½" × 8" sheets, which are used for making *kimbap* (*sushi* in Japan).[2] The laver sheet is also seasoned with sesame oil on both sides, toasted to crispness over fire, and cut into four equal pieces. Onto each piece is placed a spoonful of rice and a drop of soy sauce; the sheet is rolled around the rice and eaten. Laver is also used as a garnish by tearing it into small pieces for soup and other dishes. Kelp, dried or fresh, is used for making soup. Before using it, kelp is washed and rinsed many times; then it is cut into small pieces and sauteed in sesame oil usually with chopped clams, or other kinds of shellfish, onto which is added water and soy sauce. Soup made of kelp is preferred by many Koreans, particularly women after childbirth, because it is regarded as rich in iodine and iron.

Korea has a wide variety of fruits such as apples, peaches, pears, plums, persimmons, grapes and tangerines. They are eaten mostly as snacks, not usually as part of meals.

Many parents reported that their Korean-born children prefer their native foods to American foods. It appears that whether or not they have access to them largely depends on their parents. If the parents understand the child's needs and are interested in trying foods of another culture, they try to learn to cook Korean dishes and prepare them on special days such as the child's birthday, or go out to Korean restaurants.

When we talk about food we generally consider two aspects—the kind of food materials and how they are prepared. Different cultures prepare the same kind of materials in different ways. For instance, the way rice is cooked in the United States and in Korea is considerably different. Koreans cook rice soft, while Americans cook rice hard. Sometimes, they have rice seasoned with *Kochoo'jang* or soy sauce, while Americans sometimes have it prepared with milk or sugar. So the contrast between ways in which rice is served in both countries is also great. Vegetables, too, are cooked differently in the two cultures. In the United States, vegetables are generally overcooked; spinach, for example, is often cooked to the point of shapeless green mush. They are usually seasoned with butter and salt. In Korea, vegetables are cooked light and crisp, seasoned with soy sauce or roasted sesame seed, or garnished with sesame oil or *kochoo'jang*. Many parents reported their children did not like vegetables prepared in an American way. On the other hand, many found their children liked noodle dishes, although some did not like spaghetti with tomato sauce. In Korea noodles are often prepared with beef or chicken broth, invariably seasoned with soy sauce or hot sauce and garnished with sliced meat and chopped vegetables (scallion, onion, cucumber, etc.)

Regardless of what American foods the children liked or disliked, consensus is that they had large appetites. One mother said of their 8-year-old girl, " ... of all the food Ann wolfed down—five man-sized slices of ham, three helpings of mashed potatoes, two helpings of green bean casserole, and pickles beyond counting ... her appetite never ends. She may eat a can of Campbell's soup for breakfast all by herself. Truly, she still outeats all of us, even when we are gorging ourselves on special foods." One can safely guess that the big appetites these children have are probably a result of their having gone hungry at times. They may lack sufficient protein to replenish the energy they expend in coping with the stresses and constant activities of their new lives in the United States.

In view of the differences between the American and Korean diet, adoptive parents may wonder what to feed their child when he first arrives. Considering his past diet and foods readily available in the United States, the following ideas may be helpful. Parents may feed babies soy formula or goat milk (since some children may develop allergies to cow milk), cream of rice ceral, and grated apple or pureed apple sauce. Older children could have oatmeal, fruit, puffed wheat or rice cereal with milk, or boiled instead of fried eggs. Suggestions for lunch and supper, besides plain cooked rice and dill pickles, might include chicken or beef broth with small amounts of meat, or soup made of soybean paste (available in any Oriental food store) mixed with water, with diced onions, scallions, or soybean curd. They will probably enjoy a variety of vegetables, especially spinach, lightly cooked and seasoned with soy sauce (Kikoman), hot sauce or sesame oil (seasoning), and will surely like dill pickles. The most important thing for parents to remember is that fat- and protein-rich American foods such as cow's milk and other dairy products, fat-rich hamburger and other prepared meats, should be introduced to the child's diet gradually.

Table Manners

Standards of good table manners are different from one culture to another. Traditionally, in the United States, dinner time is a time to eat, but also a family social hour when each tells the other about what he did that day and listens to what others did. However, the custom of eating together is gradually changing, especially with families whose members engage in different activities and cannot always have meals together. Still, when they eat together, because of the tradition which stresses the social aspect of dinner, good table manners are emphasized. Young children are taught to hold forks and knives properly, handling them quietly, participate in the family conversation, or remain seated until others finish their meal. If a child has to leave the table before the group has finished, he is expected to have good reason to do so, and to ask to be excused from the table.

In Korea, however, dinner time in the family is primarily a time to eat. Traditionally, the family members often eat at separate times, as well as in separate places. Father/husband may eat alone at a small table in his own room. Wife/mother may eat alone in another room with her children. This custom is gradually changing today among younger generations in large cities; they eat together more often, whether at separate tables or at one large table. But the traditional way still persists in most parts of the country. The lack of socialization among the family members at dinner time is no doubt a result of the strict social structure and sex division imposed on the family members, between parents and children, wives and husbands, etc. This point will be discussed more fully in Chapter 3, "Social Structure."

Because of the lack of emphasis on the social aspect of dinner time in the family, no particular table manners are taught to the children as in the United States. They are expected to eat quickly and in silence. They are not supposed to waste time while eating, but to concentrate on whatever they eat. Thus, eating in silence is desired and encouraged. If a child talks, his mother may say, "If you talk while eating, food will fall out of your mouth." Eating in silence, however, often leads to fast and noisy eating. Undoubtedly, the custom of eating in silence is closely related to the general value system of Confucian culture, which does not stress socialization between the members of the family. Related to this is also the frequently used maxim: "Speech is silver, silence is gold."

American parents who are not familair with Confucian culture may naturally wonder why the child eats quickly, noisily and in silence, often head down, not participating in the family conversation. One American mother made an observation on the table manners of their adopted sons. "When they first came, they gobbled foods up quickly in silence, often slurped and chewed loudly, and would leave the table with everybody still finishing their meal. We had many talks about table manners and tried to teach them that in America, during dinner time, everyone participates in the conversation and waits until others finish their meal." Another mother who adopted two girls said, "The girls would draw up their knees on their chairs and had a hard time keeping their feet on the floor." Whenever the family went out to dinner at a restaurant, the mother had to remind them, "Remember, in public you should have good manners. Try not to draw up your feet on your chairs but keep them on the floor." The children had acquired their habits in their past culture, where they had their meals sitting on the floor at a low table, with their knees drawn up or under them.

To unlearn old habits takes time. Once the parents understand the child's past culture and customs, it helps them understand better the reasons behind their children's table manners. Thereby they can have a better perspective from which to teach them American ways of good table manners.

Sleeping

The kind of sleeping arrangements to which the child is conditioned is a part of the total childhood experience that influences the development of his personality. Anthropologist Ruth Benedict writes in *Patterns of Culture*, "The life-history of the individual is first and foremost an accommodation to the patterns and standards traditionally handed down in his community. From the moment of his birth the customs into which he is born shape his experience and behavior. By the time he can talk, he is the little creature of his culture, and by the time he is grown and able to take part in its activities, its habits are his habits, its beliefs his beliefs, its impossibilities his impossibilities. Every child that is born into his group will share them with him, and no child born into one on the opposite end of the globe can even achieve the thousandth part."[3]

Sleeping customs are often determined by the structure of the houses people live in. Today, in Korea, modern apartment buildings and houses comparable to American housing are visible in large cities. However, traditionally and still largely in the rural areas, the majority of Koreans live in houses which are markedly different from the structure of an American house. The traditional house is surrounded by a high fence in which a gate serves as the entrance door. A typical house has two or three rooms, a porch-like wooden floor in front of the rooms, a kitchen on either the left- or right-hand side, a storage room and outdoor toilet. Before setting foot on the wooden floor which leads to the rooms, a person takes off his shoes and leaves them on the ground. In winter, the room is warmed by the heat coming from the concrete floor which has a passage through which fire travels from the cookstove in the kitchen to the chimney, located in the back of the house. The floor of the room is pasted with oil-treated, sturdy paper which is waterproof, usually yellow and glossy. People sit on the floor with or without cushions, so there is no need for chairs. Furniture mainly consists of dressers, bureaus, study desk or sewing machine. Dinner tables are low, so require no chairs. When they are not in use, they are often folded away in the closet or on the shelf. At bedtime, the rooms are cleaned and thick cotton pads and quilts are spread on the floor; in the morning they are rolled up and put away in the closet.

In Korea, traditionally and even today, infants, toddlers, and even school-age children often sleep with their mothers at night, especially if the child has no siblings or is the youngest. During the daytime, whenever the child cries, the mother quickly picks him up and nurses him, cuddles him on her lap or carries him on her back. Korean mothers nurse their children on demand rather than on a fixed time schedule. In addition, the nursing period tends to be longer in Korea than in the United States. However, an exception to the rule can occur when the mother gives birth to another child soon after the first one, since she rarely has enough milk to feed two children. When the mother attends to household chores, goes shopping or visits friends or relatives, she may carry her child on her back or leave him with a grandmother or a sister who also carries him on the back.

The child may take his nap while being carried in this way or when he falls asleep, his mother may place him on the bed and may leave him. Mothers with leisure may lie down with the sleeping baby or read a book or sew sitting beside him. Children are often carried on the back even though they are able to walk, or are led by the hand while walking in the street. The close, sustained physical contacts the child experiences with adults tend to foster strong dependency. This point will be further elaborated in Chapter 2, "Emotional Adjustments."

Many adoptive mothers reported that their child asked to sleep with them or to be held and cuddled in their arms. An adoptive mother said that during the first week or so their 4-year-old girl wanted to sleep with her or to be carried in her arms all the time. For some children, the desire to sleep with someone will persist long after they have been in the United States. A single mother who adopted a 6-year-old boy said, "He (now 9 years old) still prefers to sleep with others and occasionally asks to sleep with me or his grandmother."

Some parents who had heard or read about the custom of sleeping on the floor prepared both bed and sleeping bag for their child before he arrived. One mother, who, at the suggestion of a friend, prepared a sleeping bag for her 4-year-old girl, lay beside her on the floor the first night until she fell asleep, then went to sleep on her bed. Another mother, who found it necessary to take their newly arrived 7-year-old daughter into their own bed, said, "The first night Susan had a very difficult time sleeping. She finally fell asleep at 3:30 a.m. with me, while my husband slept in a sleeping bag in the living room. She just didn't want to sleep alone. For the next five nights she slept with either me alone or with my husband and me." The girl slept with her Korean mother up until the day she left for the United States.

One mother, who had no sleeping problems with their 7-year-old boy, said, "I believe the fact that we gave him a bed near the floor and let him sleep in the same room with his new brother was a big factor in his peace of mind at bedtime. Also, we had sent pictures of his bedroom so it wouldn't be strange to him. It really helped David to have pictures of us and our home. Those pictures were important to him. He carried them everywhere with him for a while."

Needless to say, the child's sleeping adjustments, like any others, depend on his individual personality or circumstances. Some children may sleep well in a bed or on the floor, alone or with others. However, since parents do not know much of the child's personality in the beginning, it is advisable that they try to make sleeping arrangements similar to the general customs of the country in which he grew up. Since the child is accustomed to sleeping on the floor, he may be given a choice between the floor or the bed. In the case of siblings it would be a good idea, as some parents have done, to put them in a double bed or twin beds in the same room.

However, more important than whether the child sleeps on the floor or in bed is that he be allowed to sleep with another person, at least for the first night or so. In Korea no child sleeps alone. The presence of another person in the room would give him great comfort and peace of mind, especially during the first week in the United states, when he experiences great anxiety due to change of culture and grief caused by separation from his relatives. For such a child, sleeping alone at first night or two may prove to be a most traumatic experience.

2
Emotional
Adjustments

Trauma of Separation

As in the popular saying, man does not live by bread alone. Man has emotional needs that must be met by his family or someone close to him. When he is suddenly cut off from an emotional tie, he invariably suffers the trauma of separation. Various studies in child welfare and mental health show an abundance of evidence that if a person is subjected to sudden separation from his loved ones, he is likely to suffer grief, anxiety, or both. Examples of suffering from the trauma of separation are abundant in all walks of life. In an extreme case a man bereft of his wife may lose his will to live and gradually atrophy to a state of vegetation. In a less extreme situation a foster child when transferred to another home may show marked signs of stress. Even an average child who is sent away to a summer camp for the first time may experience mild unhappiness from being away from his parents.

Then there is the case of Asian children who come to the United States to be adopted by American couples. Their emotional needs may seem far greater and more complex than those of other children. Many are older than four or five, and have had a close relationship with someone—their mother or other adults. No doubt, at their departure from their homeland or from close relatives, most children experience some emotions, most probably a mixture of sadness, uncertainty, anxiety or hope. Often, however, the real impact of separation does not hit them until after they have arrived in their new homes, and face the realities of a new language and culture.

Separation from one's familiar environment taxes one with acute anxiety and grief. Claudia Jewett writes in *Adopting the Older Child*, "Even if the child has come from a home that seems neglectful, or even harmful, it was familiar to him. Being taken from it means a collapse of everything the child has known, the death of all he has accepted and trusted. He is plunged headlong into what Sigmund Freud calles 'the work of mourning.' . . . Though painful, the work of mourning is necessary before the child can come to love his new parents. If grief is not expressed and worked through, it goes underground and leaves a lasting inability to be involved except at very superficial levels."[1]

The majority of parents reported that their child sobbed the night of his arrival, the following nights, or much later. It seems that while the children submerged grief during the daytime under the pressure of activities, they usually expressed it in the evening, particularly at bedtime. One mother said, "The first few nights he sobbed softly after going to bed, but responded to my comforting. He had been separated from his family for some time before he came and I feel he had come to terms with his grief. His orphanage experience seemed to be mostly bad. He seems very happy to be here and a part of our family."

But it can take a longer time for some children to come to terms with their grief of separation. According to what some children reported, their grief was deep and lasted long, often beyond the understanding of their new parents. One 16-year-old girl who came here at age 12 said, "When I first came here, I cried every night for two weeks, looking at pictures of my Korean family. My American parents couldn't figure out why I was crying. They thought I'd be very happy because I had a piano and two cats." Needless to say, the trauma of separation these children go through calls for special understanding and for interpretation to adoptive parents.

How can parents help the child come to terms with his grief? One way to help him is to encourage him to write to his birth mother or someone close, as well as to encourage him to verbalize his feelings about his past and present experiences. Quite a few parents encouraged the child to write his birth mother or relatives. One mother who adopted an 11-year-old girl said, "Joan still loves her birth mother very much and misses her. If I were in her place, I'd certainly want to write her and want to hear from her. So it's only fair that she has the opportunity to write her birth mother. In fact, when she wasn't writing, it bothered me and made me wonder why she wasn't. She couldn't really talk about why, until something came up. Then she told me she had forgotten the Korean language. So she wrote her letter in English and sent it to the social agency to be translated into Korean and mailed to her mother." Another mother said, "It wasn't the first night, but in the following days, I told her that if she missed her uncle and felt like writing to him, she could do so. We sent the letter through the agency as we were supposed to do, but we didn't hear from her uncle for six months. So we mailed another letter directly to him. Soon after that we received a letter from him."

In cases like this, where letters were exchanged through the agencies, some took many weeks or even months to reach their destination. In some cases letters were apparently never delivered. Knowing or fearing this might happen, some children wrote to their relatives directly from the very beginning. One 19-year-old girl who came here at age 12 said, "My Mom always writes me, 'Be good to your American parents and listen to them. Behave yourself. Do go to school, of course, and study hard and do your best. Always think about your future.' She really kept me going."

When the child has no communication with his relatives, in addition to his inability to communicate with his new parents in English, he is likely to experience a great deal more anxiety and grief. According to a mother who adopted an 8-year-old child, the child had not expressed an outward sign of grief until after she had been in her new home a few weeks. One evening, she began to express her grief of separation. Her mother reports: "When she went to bed, she was weepy. Then she asked me to lie down with her, and she started to cry. For a long, painful half hour she wept, openly and hard, sobbing deep sobs over and over; stopping to blow her nose or reach out to my husband or me, or to take a drink. After calming down a little, she began to cry again, racked with sobs . . . and insisted that there had been a war in Korea, that her mother, brother and friends were all dead."

The child's emotional reactions and reasoning did not occur in a vacuum of reality. According to the mother, within a few weeks of her arrival, the child had written letters to her mother, but when she had not heard from her she was prompted to think there had been a war in her native land and everyone had been killed. To help alleviate her anxiety and grief, her mother suggested she talk to a Korean friend of the family. Her mother observed that her telephone conversation lasted for 40 minutes and soon after that "Her mood, voice, and body relaxed, and she became vibrant and playful."

If a child is deprived of sufficient help and understanding in this area, he may suffer greatly. One 14-year-old girl of mixed parentage, who had serious difficulties in her new home, came to my attention. In counseling with her, I learned that since her arrival here she had written several letters to her mother through the agencies without hearing from her. She said tearfully, "I miss my mother. I'm so sad and miserable—because my mother doesn't answer my letters." Someone adivsed her to write a diary and thereby release some of her frustrations, but apparently that didn't help her greatly. It appears that what she needed most was to have some contact with her birth mother from whom she could have received some kind of emotional support until she had established a secure relationship with her new parents. In the case of this girl, there are indications that the agencies had not actively facilitated the exchange of letters between the girl and her mother. Because of this she developed severe anxiety and grief which appeared to have contributed to much of her difficulties in her new home.

According to a few parents, in the early 1970's the social agencies advised them not to allow children to have contact with their birth mothers. Some of the reasons were that the contact would create problems for adoptive parents, which in turn meant problems for the agencies. As a result, children's needs had been neglected. If the agencies allowed contact at all, it was through them.

One family who adopted a 7-year-old girl had a relatively easy transition, largely due to understanding and wise handling by her parents, with the help of a counselor. This child had a particularly close relationship with her birth mother. In the first week after her arrival in her new home, the child sobbed every night at bedtime and tried to communicate something to her parents with her ten fingers. The baffled mother did not understand what the child was trying to say and sought help from a counselor. The child sobbed into the telephone, "I'm dying to see my mom. I'm going back to home with six more nights. My mother will move soon to a new place. If I don't go back soon I won't be able to find her. My mother was crying when I left at the airport. Let me go! Let me go!"

When a child's need to go back to her mother is as intense as this, it is best to encourage and allow her to write to her mother. This will give her the opportunity to express some of her grief and anxiety due to the separation. When the girl was encouraged to write to her mother, she wrote how much she missed her and pleaded with her mother to let her come home. She even promised she would show her mother the new pair of shoes and boots her adoptive parents bought for her and that she would give her all the allowances she had saved. When she wrote a letter to her mother, her face glowed with the emotion generated in the act of writing the letter. After she had written the letter, she became relaxed and playful.

That evening, according to her mother, the child volunteered to sleep in her bed for the first time in the entire week since her arrival. In the succeeding days, waiting for a letter from her mother and confident that her mother would let her come home, she began to relax. After a while, she became more receptive to learning the English her mother taught her, as well as going to school. She has since made rapid progress with her English, and has become an integral part of the family. However, like almost all children, she has completely forgotten the Korean language, and has lost the need to write to her birth mother. According to her American parents, the fact that the birth mother still writes to the child is acceptable to them. In this case, the parents receptiveness to the child's need, coupled with their empathy toward the birth mother, has greatly contributed to the child's coming to terms with her grief and entering a positive relationship with her new parents.

Jacquelin McCoy writes in her article, "Identity As a Factor in the Adoptive Placement of the Older Child," in *Child Welfare*: "The child's feelings about his background and his separation from his natural parents continue through his life, and although they may be worked through to a greater or lesser extent, they will crop up again from time to time. The important thing is that the child be free enough of his investment in his family to allow himself to enter into a new situation and gradually take on new parents. Once new relationships are formed and new indentifications made, the thoughts and feelings he has about his beginnings will be less threatening. As he has newer, more positive experiences, the old ones become less important in his day-to-day living."[2]

If the cases discussed here teach us something, it

seems that we cannot underestimate the importance of recognizing the child's need to communicate with his birth mother and to release the stressful emotions built up by the separation and change of culture. If parents can understand this and facilitate such communication, they can greatly aid the child in adjusting to his new home and strengthening his bond with his new family. If such a contact is not possible for some children, it is advisable that they be given an opportunity to talk to someone, ideally an adult who understands their language. These avenues of communication not only give them a chance to release their stressful emotions, but also help the parents and social workers learn something about what the children think and feel at the moment. This will help them assess their children's immediate needs. Often making an accurate assessment of a child's needs at this time, and meeting them satisfactorily, can mean minimum trauma for the child. Otherwise, it can make his future adjustment more difficult. Thus, successful handling of a child's initial needs cannot be overemphasized.

Regression

It is generally held as true that if a child is subjected to enormous stress, he may likely regress to an earlier behavior. In the cases where a child is transposed to a new culture, language and unfamiliar environment, he is subjected to enormous stress and may express his stress in regressive behavior.

A mother described the regressive behavior of her 8-year-old girl in this way. "This morning she awoke early and came crawling on her hands and knees to the kitchen. Then she climbed into my lap, saying her cute 'Goodmarh-ning.' She snuggled up to me warmly and at the same time drank in all the fondling and kisses that I showered her with. . . . In her feigned crying, she is in a way returning to her infancy with me; I feel I am at a crib picking up a baby, loving her before starting on the child's day of activity. . . . Sometimes I feel she behaves very much like a three- or four-year-old. . . ."

Needless to say, the child's behavior is an extreme form of regression, which is no doubt the result of the enormous stress she was subjected to, due to the change of culture. Furthermore, her regression seems to have been induced by the way her mother treated her. It can be explained in terms of the differences of the child's past and present culture, and her confused emotional reaction to them. When she was young, chances are that she had been greatly indulged by her Korean mother, usually up to the age of six, which is the cultural norm. Then, when the child came to the United States, she was eight years old and had already passed the stage of being indulged by the Korean norm. But her American mother, anxious to make the girl feel loved, cuddled her on her lap, following the Korean custom that she heard about, and also kissed and hugged her according to the American custom. In the child's eye, her mother's way of treating her was similar to that of her Korean mother who indulged her when she was preschool-age. Thus she might have felt it was acceptable for her to behave as she did.

Marjorie Margolies, a mother who adopted two girls, one from Korea and another from Vietnam, and author of *They Came to Stay*, writes that her 6-year-old girl of Korean background asked her one day to suckle her breasts.[3] Such a behavior may seem rather an extreme form of regression, but understandable in terms of enormous stress to which the child was subjected. But one may ask, "Why this form of regression?" In the United States the instance of a child of 5- or 6-year-old wanting to suckle her mother's breast is unusual, if not rare, no matter how much stress the child may have been subjected to. It can therefore be explained in the context of the culture from which the child came. In Korea, such a behavior is frequently observed among young children, largely because, traditionally, almost all babies are breast-fed. In addition, mothers tend to indulge their children a great deal up to age six and even beyond that age. Often a child of three or four or even older, particularly if he is an only child or the youngest in the family, is permitted to suckle or fondle his mother's breasts. Furthermore, children who were deprived of the gratification of early dependency needs by their mothers may tend to do the same. There is some indication that the child of the author Margolies was deprived of the gratification of such a dependency need early in life because her mother had been bed-ridden with tuberculosis.[4]

Ways of Expressing Affection

One of the most basic human needs is to love and be loved. Yet, the culture we live in largely defines what love is and how it is to be expressed or not to be expressed.

Perhaps one of the greatest cultural differences between East and West is the way in which people in both worlds express affection. Universally, affection is expressed by some kind of physical and verbal means, but the form and quality of the expression is vastly different from one culture to another. The American way of affection is more active and direct, and essentially geared to strengthen the ego of the individual and therefore his independence. American parents kiss and hug their children daily as a token of affection—when they put them to bed at night or send them away to school or when they return home. Moreover, parental kisses and hugs are often accompanied by the verbal expression, "I love you."

In contrast, the Eastern expression of affection is passive and indirect, and fosters dependency. For instance, Korean mothers rarely kiss or hug their children. Instead, they cuddle the child a great deal in their arms or on their laps or carry him on their backs strapped with a quilt, as a token of affection. These passive physical contacts provide the child with warmth and a sense of security, but neither stimulate feelings nor the need to respond.

Many parents reported that in the beginning the child just tolerated their kissing or hugging and did not respond to it. Some children actively shrank away from it. One mother described her first meeting with their 8-year-old girl at the airport. "While we waited to check with social workers about taking her home, I held her hand in that jammed crowd and kissed it. Twice she took her hand out of mine." Another mother said of their 7-year-old boy, "We noticed that it was hard for John to be affectionate. We had to make an effort to hug and kiss him. He liked it, but it was a long time before he could do that back to us. Even now, it is hard for him to demonstrate his feeling in an affectionate way. Once in a while I will find him in back of me rubbing and that is a 'wow' experience." Korean parents often ask their child to rub their backs or arms or legs. Probably the boy rubbed his mother's back and learned that it was a way to please her.

On the other hand, a majority of the children interviewed suggested that when they were kissed or hugged by their American parents they felt uncomfortable. One 15-year-old boy who came here at age 11 said, "My Mom kissed me and hugged me when I went to school or out to play. I felt strange and didn't know what to do. I just stood there. That was the way she showed her affection to me. So I had to show my love in the same way. I guess I kissed her back after I had been here for sometime." For some children, it will take some years to learn to respond to kissing or hugging. One mother who adopted an 11-year-old girl said, "Joan didn't want to be hugged or kissed or sit on my lap when she first came here. She didn't want to be touched. She was very cold. This last year (after she's been in America four years) she will hold my hands or give a good-night hug, but she always has to take the initiative. Even now when we try to give her a hug, she sort of stiffens up and doesn't like it. Sometimes when she feels the need or desire to give us a hug or hold hands, we feel it a special treat, because she wants to do it."

In a few cases, the child's witnessing of adults kissing or hugging produced some strong reactions in him. One mother who adopted two brothers at age 10 and 8 said, "Whenever they saw a man and a woman kissing and hugging on televison, they would cover their faces with their hands or run and hide behind the door. It was such a riot!" Another mother reported that one day when she and her husband were hugging and kissing in the living room, their 6-year-old boy came over and said, "Daddy, don't hurt mommy." Apparently, the boy thought they were fighting because he had often witnessed his foster parents physically fighting in the homes where he had lived.

Many parents reported that, while their children were unresponsive to their kissing and hugging, they readily responded to an invitation to sit on their laps or to be carried on their backs. A mother said of their 5-year-old boy, "Whenever relatives or friends visited, he would climb into their lap or snuggle up to them. We told him not to unless he were invited to do so. He would also cling to their arms or put his head on their shoulders."

In the two cultures, not only are the physical expressions of affection different, but also the verbal expressions. American parents verbalize their feelings of affection a great deal to their children and do so directly—"I love you." One of the first words children learn from their parents is "love." One 18-year-old girl, an orphan who came here at age 12 said, "My American parents have shown me how to love. They love me and I love them. There is a lot of affection and love between us. In America people express their affection more than Koreans do. In Korea I loved my little sisters and grandma, but I didn't experience many feelings of love. Life was simple; we lived without feeling much about many things."

In Korea, a mother rarely expresses her feelings of love directly to her children, in the words of "I love you," although she may say indirectly "The mother loves you." Generally speaking, the word "love" is rarely used in daily conversation. If the word "love" is expressed, it is when a mother exhorts her child—"You must love your brother or sister" or "You must love your country."

One 19-year-old girl who has been in America 7 years said "Even now, I don't know why . . . but it's not easy for me to say to my parents, 'I love you,' although I can say it in a card or a letter. My kind of love is silent love. It's not easily expressed verbally." Her early upbringing is still influencing the way she feels, but other factors also seem to be involved in her case, such as her personality and her relationship with her parents.

How does a Korean mother express her feeling of love verbally to her child? She expresses it indirectly, often by way of solicitous concern and care. Thus the child learns to equate solicitous concern and care with expressions of love. From his field work in a Japanese fishing community, Edward Norbeck reported that the Japanese child also received solicitous care.[5] This is not surprising, because Japanese child care is essentially similar to that of Korean or Chinese, largely because of their shared tradition of Confucianism which fosters strong dependency. Solicitous concern and care are a by-product of dependency culture. A 17-year-old girl, an only child who was greatly indulged by her birth mother, cited an example of maternal love she received in the past. When she was sick in bed, her birth mother stayed by her bedside and spoonfed her, coaxing "eat more."

Thus, children who have learned affection by way of solicitous concern and care are likely to expect this form of affection from their American parents. A 19-year-old girl who came here at age 11 said, "If someone is not feeling good or is unhappy, you can tell it. If I was pouting, my parents never came and asked me what was the matter. They just left me alone to take care of my own problems. I wanted affection from my parents, but I didn't get it. So that was painful."

By the same token, children may express affection by solicitous concern and care, which may either delight or annoy their parents, depending on their personalities or how the concern is expressed. One mother described her 8-year-old girl, "She was free to be in grandma's arms, and she often snuggled up to her. It was as though she had always known her grandma. What thrilled me most was the way she responded to the fact that grandma's legs hurt and she can't walk fast. When we went shopping, she held grandma's hand on the street, and walked right with her. She was concerned with her at the curb, and wouldn't try to hurry in the usual fashion of a lively child. At dinner in the evening, she helped grandma on with her sweater and was obviously being solicitous of an elder." Another mother said of her 10-year-old girl, "She is aware of every kind of mood I'm in. If I appear tired, she will say, 'Mom, you look tired. Go to bed.' Or when she thinks I'm unhappy or troubled, she makes a point of finding out why. She is so thoughtful and concerned, not carefree."

Similarly, Jan de Hartog, an adoptive father of two girls and author of *The Children*, writes, "Marjorie and I discussed that this uncanny awareness of our moods and thought gradually took on a more positive aspect, expressing itself in an occasional unchildlike concern for our welfare. It was pretty disconcerting the first time to hear my older daughter, aged six, say one evening before supper, 'Daddy, you look tired. Sit down here and read the paper. I'll get your glasses for you.' As I obeyed, baffled and delighted, I felt all the same that slight uneasiness again. Was it natural, I asked myself, for a child of her age to be so solicitous."[6]

The negative reactions of parents to solicitous concern can be understood in terms of American value systems which put an emphasis on self-sufficiency and privacy. In general, American parents try to keep their worries or troubles to themselves and do not like to be questioned about their inner thoughts, moods or welfare, particularly by a child whom they expect to be carefree. On the other hand, the child's behavior can be understood in terms of what she had learned from her birth mother about expressing affection through solicitous concern and care.

Plethora of Expression

The fact that a Korean child is brought up being cradled on the lap or carried on the back tends to foster physical passivity in the child. In addition, emotional passivity is fostered by strong parental authority and lack of sufficient verbal give-and-take between the child and his mother. This conditioning of both physical and emotional passivity neither stimulates emotions nor facilitates their release. As a result, the child learns to suppress whatever feelings he has and grows up underdeveloped in his ability to express and respond. Such conditioning is undoubtedly designed to make the child more amenable to the status quo, rather than to induce him to change it. The only times when the child is likely to express his feelings or to respond are when he is compelled by excessive internal or external pressure, and when he feels safe doing so. Therefore, the child learns to handle his emotions by either suppression or explosion. To which side he swings at a given moment depends on his personality and the immediate situation.

When the child thus conditioned phsycially and emotionally is placed in an American home, he encounters a great deal of affective stimulus such as kissing and hugging, as well as constant encouragement to express emotions or to participate in activities. To this the child is likely to respond either by shrinking away from over-stimulation or responding in excess, depending on his personality. However, sooner or later, he will learn to express his emotions and not to suppress them. This process will naturally bring out feelings that had been suppressed in the past, but also those that are being stimulated by the American culture. Since he had not been brought up in American culture and had not learned to express and respond in the way considered proper by American standards, the child will likely express his emotions in excess.

Some parents may view an excess of expression on the part of the child as a desperate craving for affection after "a lifetime's starvation of affections." Jan de Hartog writes in *The Children*, "Once you, his mother, have cleared this hurdle and his strinking from physical contact is over (the older the child, the longer this will take), you will suddenly find yourself confronted with a hunger on his part for physical closeness, so ravenous and insatiable that chances are you may end by being seriously worried whether there isn't something psychologically wrong with him. . . . I have not heard of a single exception to this rule: all children from Korea or Vietnam are literally starved for affection; once they surrencer themselves to you, there is no moderation or restraint until their desperate craving is satisfied and they have made up in the space of a few months for the emotional deprivation of a life time."[7]

No doubt many of the children may have suffered lack of affection by American standards, and even their needs on various developmental stages inadequately met. However, as already discussed, the cultural standards and ways of dealing with emotions are different in East Asia and America. Because of this difference, the child's excessive response may be explained in view of his past conditioning and his present environment in his American home. If the child had not been brought to the United States and had not been stimulated emotionally he would probably have grown up and lived under Confucian and other cultural constraints, without ever realizing what American parents may consider emotional deprivation. Whatever deprivation he may had had by American standards, he would have lived without it ever seriously hindering his life, because his culture does not ask much of him in the way of emotional expression or response.

The child's excessive response is also in large part due to the enormous frustrations to which he has been subjected, due to the change of culture. The child has to learn new ways of doing things and unlearn the old. Some children will express this frustration in torrents of physical activities. One mother described the way their 8-year-old child went through this process: "We are dizzied by her constant activity, her running, jumping, teasing, playing, hugging, hitting. When she pummels her father there is an occasional sock. At times she comes on like a tank, physically and emotionally. We are guessing that in her confusion and frustration she acts out her feelings, being rough with books, and verging on being hurtful to the rest of us."

Once the emotional reservoir is emptied, and through the gradual process of socialization in the United States, the child will learn new ways of coping with his energy and possibly achieve moderation, neither totally inhibiting nor totally outpouring. Until such times, however, many children will probably have to go through the tumbling stages from inhibition to a plethora of expression.

3
Social
Structure

Every society is organized by some kind of social structure, most often according to its religious or ethical system. In China, Japan and Korea, Confucianism has served for centuries as the essential basis for its ethical, social, cultural and political life.

The foundation of Confucianism is the dictum on the so-called "five cardinal relationships" between father and son, wife and husband, elder and younger brother, friend and friend, ruler and subject. The dictum decrees that these relationships, except that between friends, are inherently unequal: the husband is superior to his wife by virtue of sex, the father is superior to his son and the elder brother to the younger by virtue of age, and ruler is superior to his subjects by virtue of status. In this framework of relationships, where there are only superiors and inferiors, a superior holds absolute authority over an inferior, at least in theory if not always in practice; an inferior is expected to obey his superior unconditionally. From this absolute premise the Confucian society is organized. This is why the concept of equality before God or supreme law or the value of human rights (or individual rights) has never evolved in the tradition of Confucianism.

In this system the worth of a person is primarily determined by sex, age, or social status, not by the intrinsic value of life or the individual himself. As a result, a person is a mere denominator of superior or inferior in a relationship. A strong emphasis on the hierarchy of a relationship, as well as on the family group rather than the individual, is built into many aspects of Confucian culture. For example, in Korea as in Japan and China, one's family name precedes one's personal name.

Perhaps the most important example of the effects of Confucian culture is language. In Korean, as in Japanese, it is not essential for a sentence to indicate a subject, possessive pronoun, or indirect object. As a result, these elements are often omitted in daily conversaton. The function of a Korean verb is also drastically different from that of an English verb. A Korean verb comes at the end of a sentence, and changes forms, according to the status of the speaker in relation to the listener. These points will be fully discussed in Chapter 6, "Language."

Husband-Wife Relationship

According to the Confucian dictum, a husband is superior to his wife by virtue of his sex, and entitled to have absolute authority over her. The male authority is further reinforced by the Confucian tenet—"the Path of Three Obediences"—which says: "A girl must obey her father as a child, her husband as a wife, and her son as a widow." This tenet, along with the Confucian dictum, has laid the foundation for male supremacy in East Asia, wherever Confucianism has been adopted as the basis of their culture. Thus Confucianism gave Eastern men a formidable ground from which they could trample their women for centuries.

Although today women have the right to vote, and more women than ever before are college educated and work in their chosen professions, their number is small and limited to urban areas. Only a few decades ago the majority of parents did not believe in education for their daughters. This meant that very few girls went to school, especially beyond primary school. As a result, they had no means of support, except to marry and be supported by their husbands or by their sons in old age. To prepare them for such a life, parents taught their daughters obedience and docility as feminine virtues so that they would be amenable to male authority. Parents often arranged marriages for their daughters to suit family needs. Girls had no say about their choice of their husbands.

Because the female was inferior to the male, the husband had the right to demand total obedience from his wife. He talked down to her and behaved toward her in a dictatorial manner, which often verged on tyranny. The wife waited on her husband hand and foot, and often ate after he had finished his meal. Although some of the younger generation today may not exactly follow the old master-servant pattern of a husband-wife relationship, much of the tradition still persists because the pattern is deeply ingrained in the basic aspects of the culture.

Today as well as in the past, when a woman marries she keeps her maiden name, not so much because her independence is respected, but because she is an outsider. Furthermore, husband and wife rarely address one another by thier personal names, for several reasons. First, according to the Confucian dictum, husband and wife are not equal in status. Secondly, when they were children, they were always addressed by their relational names by their inferiors, but by the personal names by their superiors. Thus personal names are associated with low status and childhood. Since marriage supposedly grants adult status, married persons may not wish to be addressed by their personal names. The other side of the coin is that names, particularly personal names, are considered sacred. Thus the husband, even though he is superior to his wife, is reluctant to address her by her personal name. Instead, husband and wife address one another by the term *yŏbo* (hello), or a husband refers to his wife by an impersonal pronoun, *annae*, meaning the "one inside," and wife to her husband as *urijuin*, meaning "our master." However, when the couple has a child, they now begin to address or refer to each other by the child's name plus "father" or "mother," supposedly a more respectful term. Most adults who have a child prefer to be identified or addressed by others, as so-and-so's mother or father. If they have more than one child, they prefer to be identified as the mother (or father) of their oldest child. A person who doesn't have a child of his own is referred to as so-and-so's aunt or uncle. No doubt this custom is designed to reinforce the family system, but also to diminish the importance of personal names. As a result, children often do not know their mother's or their aunt's personal or family names, but know their father's name, because neighbors identify them as the son or daughter of their father.

Traditionally, in addition to her subservience to her husband, the wife's paramount duty is to give birth to a male child, because a son is needed to continue the family line and to support his parents in their old age. If there is more than one son, the oldest son assumes the duty of supporting his parents in old age and, in turn, inherits most of their property. Since female children are eventually married off to other families and do not bring benefits to the parents, they are a disappointment to their parents and are regarded as an economic and social liability. Only a few decades ago, if the wife was unable to bear a son, the husband was justified in taking a concubine into the household or letting her keep a separate household, in order to have a son. In some cases, if a husband was not satisfied with his wife for whatever reason, he could divorce her outright without a trial, merely by filing papers with the authorities, indicating his decision for a divorce. The predicament of divorced women was bleak. Today as in the past, children with divorced parents remain in the custody of their fathers and often do not have the chance to see their mother. Since the majority of women had no education or marketable skills, if their husbands died, they were often left with no means to support themselves or their children. This is why widows often surrendered their children to the city authorities (usually the police station) or to orphanages to be cared for. This was also the situation of divorced women, who often had no means to support themselves and had to return to their parents for support. But parents often discouraged their daughters from returning to them by insisting they remain in marriage regardless of hardship. Even when they had marketable skills, they often had to fight or bear social prejudice because their neighbors and others looked down on them for working outside the home.

Because of the existence of these traditional prejudices most women are forced to stay in marriage as long as their husbands keep them; thus the divorce rate has been low. Some Westerners often mistakenly attribute the low divorce rate to family stability. However, family stability as such has been achieved at the misery of countless wives who have had no alternatives but to stay in marriage.

Today under new laws passed to improve the rights of women, some wives even initiate divorce and lead independent lives. Furthermore, due to increasing job opportunities for, and changing attitudes toward working women, more women are working today outside the home. However, the majority of women still live their lives shackled by the century-old Confucian dictum on "the five cardinal relationships" and its tenet—"the Path of Three Obediences."

Father-Child Relationship

Korea is not only a husband's country, but also a father's country. Traditionally, the father assumes absolute authority over his children, demands absolute obedience from them, and administers harsh punishment to children who disobey. His authority over his child is fixed and, more or less, lasts a life time. He will always be a father and will maintain his superior position over his child. The child, whether youngster or adult, defers to his father in manner and language. As a rule, there is minimal verbal exchange between father and child. If a father talks to his child, it is usually to give him instructions, to make requests, or to exhort or scold him. As a result, their relationship tends to be distant and lacks warmth and affection.

Conditioned by such a parent-child relationship, the child tends to be quiet and inhibited in the presence of adults. One adoptive mother noted, "We have some contact with Korean people. We've noted that in the presence of Korean adults, our children sit quietly with their hands on their laps, and spoke only if spoken to. They become noticeably inhibited, while with American adults they behave more like themselves and treat adults like their pals."

The distance created by the authority-obedience relationship of father and child is further reinforced by the fact that a father almost never shares in child care or housework, such as cleaning, cooking, or washing dishes. If a man does any housework, he is an exception among many hundreds. The reason why an average Korean man is reluctant to do housework is, again, largely because of the legacy of Confucianism, in which manual work is viewed as degrading to a man's self-esteem. In contrast, most American fathers often participate in child care, as well as help with cooking and other housework. One mother said their 12-year-old girl laughed at her father because he helped with the dishes.

Even if the father-child relationship is generally distant and lacks warmth, the father tends to be more distant with his daughter than with his son. When a girl-child is placed in an American home, the father often bears the brunt of her past experience, for most likely she had no close relationships with adult males. On the other hand, in the United States, fathers do not usually play a role of dictatorial authority, but tend to be more warm and affectionate toward their children. Quite a few parents reported that in the beginning their daughter would not go near her new father and would cry if he made any attempt to hold or reach out to her. One mother reported that, during the first few weeks, her 5-year-old daughter was very fearful of her father and would cry whenever he tried to come near her or when she was left alone with him. This is most likely because the child had neither spent time with male adults nor had a warm relationship with them in the past. It will take some time for her to get used to the presence of a male adult, especially one who tends to be overly affectionate. So it would be advisable that in the beginning, the father stay in the background and let the mother play a major role in taking care of the girl-child.

On the other hand, even though they come from the same culture, some children will relate well to their American fathers from the beginning, because of such factors as personality, circumstances or age. For example, girls coming from a background in which they have some contact with American servicemen tended to be more friendly to their American fathers. A mother described how easily their 8-year-old daughter of mixed parentage related to her father, "When she sees him reading the paper she backs out of the room, and when he puts the paper down she flies into his lap."

Mother-Child Relationship

In most cultures a mother represents to her child a primary source of love. But the scheme of Confucianism makes the Korean mother devote herself even more to her child, often to the point of self-denial. Her child is everything to her, and she lives for him. One reason for this is that she has limited avenues through which she can channel her affection, other than her child. She expresses maternal love by waiting on and trying to do everything for him, often things he is capable of doing himself. In so doing, the mother fosters a strong sense of dependency in her child, which often contributes to the maintenance of a strong bond between them throughout their lives. A 19-year-old girl compared the mother-child relationship in the two cultures. "In Korea, family is much closer than here. Mothers take care of their kids more. They are always there to help you whenever you have problems. This is true even when you are older and do not live with your parents. Maybe it's different with other families, but I felt I was not being taken care of enough by my American parents. Over here, you are brought up to be independent from an early age. As soon as you become 18, you are no longer a child. You are on your own. You either go to work or college."

However, the Korean mother tends to devote herself more to a son than to a daughter. She often gives her son better food and clothing and exempts him from helping her with tasks around the house, such as cooking, doing dishes, cleaning, setting the dinner table or baby-sitting with younger siblings. By such preferential treatment, the boy-child early learns to think that the male is superior to the female and entitled to special privileges.

As a result, a boy is more likely to have a harder time than a girl in adjusting to the American way of life. It will take some time for him to realize that in the United States girls and boys are equal and American parents treat their daughters and sons equally. One mother said, "Along with language development and understanding of some of our American ways of doing things, we were able to talk to Jamie about how women and men in our culture are equal and can be anything they want to be. We also talked about the changing roles of men and women in our society. In our family Daddy cooks and helps around the house and Jamie's older sisters have outside chores as well as helping inside our home. In other words, we work together as a family on tasks. He still has problems accepting this. Hopefully, as he matures he will be able to broaden his thinking."

In addition, the boy-child may have to adjust to the fact that in America the mother's authority bears as much weight as the father's. Many mothers interviewed reported that at first their sons respected and responded better to their husbands' authority than to theirs. A mother of a 10-year-old boy, who came here at age 7, "Bill has always responded better to my husband's authority. He never outright ignored my authority, but it was difficult for him to accept direction from me. I think he still feels deep down that men are superior to women." Another mother said of their 17-year-old boy who came to them at age 9. "He respected men much more than women. He didn't respect my word or my suggestions, apparently because I was a woman. So, whenever I wanted him to get certain things done, I had to go to my husband and have him talk to him." One father said of their 16-year-old boy, "John did exactly what I told him to do, but gave my wife a considerable amount of problems when I was not around. As soon as I showed up, there were no problems."

Quite a few adoptive mothers said their sons expected to be waited on and were reluctant to help with tasks around the house, regarding that as a woman's work. One mother said their 10-year-old boy loathed setting the table and felt humiliated by doing so. Undoubtedly, the boy-child's reluctance to do housework may involve a number of factors—his past learning of Confucian attitudes toward manual work and male attitudes toward housework, as well as the way his mother excused him from helping her.

In a few cases, even some girl-children proved reluctant to do housework. One 14-year-old girl said she felt like a housemaid when she was asked to do the dishes. Her family in Korea had a *sikmo* (house-maid) who cooked, washed and cleaned. She never had to do any housework. Another girl said that when she first came here (at age 13), her mother asked her to vacuum the living room. But she was reluctant, and suggested that her mother hire a cleaning woman. Her attitude can be explained in terms of her past experiences, in which, according to her, her birth mother did all of the housework and allowed her to do only homework or play with her firends. In addition, her attitude was no doubt influenced by the value-attitudes of a people who regard manual work, as well as persons engaged in it, as lowly.

Sibling Relationships

According to the Confucian dictum on the five relationships, the elder brother is superior to the younger by virtue of age, therefore he can exercise authority over his younger brother just as his parents would. Along with this authority goes his responsibility for the younger. In turn, the younger brother is expected to respect the authority of the elder brother. One 18-year-old who came here at age 11 said, "If my elder brother asks me to do something, I do it, even if I don't want to do it. No argument. He is my elder brother, and I respect his authority because he is older than I."

This type of sibling relationship sharply contrasts with that in the United States, where siblings treat each other as equals, and the older brother does not assume authority or responsibility over the younger one as a parent would. Some parents reported that their older child tried to assume authority over the younger and, thus, created some problems. This often happened when siblings were placed together in the same home. One mother who adopted two sisters, Suzie and Ann, said, "In the beginning Suzie felt responsible for Ann and would tell her what to do. As time went on, Ann resented this. So we discouraged Suzie from bossing Ann." One family that adopted two brothers, Dick and John, gives another example. Dick, who is five years younger than John, came first; John came 5 months later, reportedly to take care of his younger brother. According to their parents, John tried to "run" Dick's life and would tell him what to do. The mother said, "I finally stepped in and said, 'John, back up. Leave Dick alone. He's been here 5 months and gets along fine. We'll take care of him. You are his brother, not his parent. Don't try to be his parents.' After that, he quit being a parent to Dick."

Furthermore, the tendency of the elder sibling to assume authority over the younger may lead him to counteract parental authority. One mother who adopted a boy and two girls said that the boy, older than the girls but not related by birth, tried to assume authority over them and wanted to be the sole speaker for them. As a result, his authority often counteracted the mother's authority about what the girls should do. The mother said, "I'd tell the girls they couldn't do certain things, but the boy would tell them they could. So I had some problems in this area."

In addition, the hierarchy of the elder-younger sibling relationship is reinforced by various cultural mechanism, notably by kinship terms. In Korea the younger siblings almost never address their elder siblings by their personal names. For example, younger brother addresses his elder borther by the term "*hyŭng-nim*" (a respectful term for elder brother) while a younger sister adresses her elder sister by the term "*ŏnni*" (elder sister). A younger brother, however, addresses his elder sister by "*nu-nim*" (a respectful term for elder sister). If there is more than one elder sister or brother in the family, the younger sibling differentiates his elder siblings by adding the modifier "big" or "small" or "first," "second," or "third" plus the term "elder sister" or "elder brother." This system of address also contrasts with that of the American, where siblings address one another by their personal names, regardless of age. One mother who adopted a 7-year-old boy wrote, "Jason remembers and speaks of his Korean family and friends, but we are puzzled that he does not remember the names of his Korean brother and sister, nor the Korean language." Since John's brother and sister are older than he, chances are that he never addressed them by their personal names. Even if the boy knew the names of his siblings, he had probably forgotten their names along with the Korean language, in the course of learning English.

One couple reported that their newly arrived 7-year-old son, John, treated their 5-year-old daughter, Mary (also adopted from Korea) as inferior. However, Mary was 18 months old when she was adopted. Two years older and male, John assumed superiority to his sister. He excluded her from games he played with his brother and ignored her overtures of friendship. The mother writes, "His aloof treatment of her was not from any personal dislike. He not only refused to kiss her goodnight, but also wouldn't let her kiss him. She did not really understand this, even though we tried to explain his reasons for acting this way. Mary is an outgoing, loving child and her feelings were hurt badly. Later, as he began to understand English, we explained to him that little sisters are just as important as his brothers in America. He accepts this to the point that they now have a brother-sister relationship that is pleasing to both of them. I might say, though, that the overall adjustment of John's adoption has affected Mary more than anyone in the family. I would almost say it has been more difficult for her than for John. John's early rejection of her was a contributing factor."

In the relationship of these siblings, there is a touch of irony. Here are two chidren who were born in the same country, and yet had spent their early childhood in two completely different cultures. By the time they met in their American home, they had almost nothing in common, culturally and emotionally, except the common racial heritage and country of their birth. Mary, having grown up in America from infancy, was really an American child by the time John met her. She tried to treat John as her equal as she would her other brother. On the other hand, John tried to treat her as an inferior as he would in Korea. Both children tried to treat the other according to the custom of the cultures in which they spent their formative years, quite innocent of the antithetical differences of the two cultures.

Relationships Between the Sexes

Standards for social behavior between the sexes are probably most contrasting in Confucian and American cultures. In Confucian tradition boys and girls are brought up in strict separation from an early age. This custom lasts more or less until old age. The custom of strict separation between the sexes is deeply rooted in the Confucian teachings, starting with the Confucian dictum on the "five cardinal relationships," which assigns superiority to the male and inferiority to the female. This is further reinforced by the Confucian precept that says, "Boys and girls must not sit together after the age of seven."

Although today there are some signs that this custom is changing in some urban segments of the country, the Confucian teaching on the male-female relationship still has a formidable hold on the mind and manner of Korean people and virtually dominates the social fabric of their lives. Traditionally and at the present time, the separation between boys and girls is strictly enforced in elementary school. In the lower grades boys and girls may share the same classroom, but the boys are seated in one side of the classroom and girls on the other. Some teachers may try to make a boy sit with a girl as punishment. One 16-year-old girl who came here at age 11 said, "Teachers would say, 'You guys keep quiet or I'll mix you boys and girls and make you sit by each other. We were just terrified by this." In the upper classes, boys and girls are grouped separately in different classrooms. In school or out, boys and girls do not play with one another. One American mother who adopted two sisters at aged 8 and 10 said, "Our girls are ill at ease in the presence of boys. They don't know how to play with boys and find it difficult to cope with their teasings."

Needless to say, the enforcement of strict division between the sexes produces an emotional distance between them and influences their behavior toward each other. For instance, when a boy and girl run into one another in school or in the street, one neither greets nor talks to the other, even though they know each other. When a child thus brought up moves to America, he or she is likely to behave in a way contrary to the American norms of behavior. One mother said she was "very upset" over an instance in which an 11-year-old girl did not respond to her boy-classmate who said "Hi" when they ran into one another in the street. The mother was upset because such a behavior is easily taken in the United States as a slight. One 16-year-old girl who came here at age 11 described the different ways in which she related to boys in Korea and the United States. "In Korea, if I ran into a boy in the street, even though I knew him, I would just look at him and pass him by without saying a word. Here in the United States, when I see a boy I know in the street, I go over and say, "Hi," or "How are you?"

On the other hand, some children of mixed parentage who had lived outside the mainstream of Korean culture and had some contact with American servicemen, tended to be more outgoing with the opposite sex. One mother observed that their 8-year-old girl was at ease with boys and enjoyed playing with them. One 19-year-old girl of the same background said that, in the small village where she grew up, she had played with girls and boys as long as she remembered. This is rather an exception to the Korean norms of behavior, but there are reasons. First, the girl's playmates were all children of mixed parentage like herself; their common background brought them together, regardless of sex. Secondly, the milieu in whcih she lived was outside the mainstream of society and more loosely structured than the rest.

In middle schools boys and girls usually go to different schools and have lesser contact with the opposite sex than before. Teenagers receive no sex education at home or in school, other than the instruction girls receive about menstruation from their mothers. Biological changes in adolescent years, as well as the emotional experiences young people go through in that period are given little attention and largely ignored. Girls rarely discuss matters of sex with others, although some girls may read about it or talk with their close girlfriends. Discussing sex-related matters is often considered in bad taste. About biological or sex-related matters, people tend to have the attitude: "Let nature take care of itself." For instance, unless others bring up the subject, married women do not talk about their pregnancies, tell when a child is expected, or send birth announcements. Pregnancy is accepted as a natural part of marriage, just as growing old is part of life. Their nonchalant attitude toward pregnancy or the birth of a child is probably also related to their general attitudes toward life or the value of life.

Traditionally, there is no dating among high school students. Parents as well as school authorities warn boys and girls that any association with the opposite sex is improper and should be avoided. Accordingly, boys and girls are rarely seen walking together in the street. There is no public display of affection between the sexes, because it is not only regarded as improper but often branded as "bad." It is not surprising that a 17-year-old adoptee was "disgusted" seeing boys and girls kissing in the hallway of her American juionr high. She censured their behavior as "bad." Her father told her, "You may not like what you see at school, but no one has the right to judge them as bad. Here in America you can be anything you want to be. No one prevents you from becoming what you want to become."

How do the youth channel their youthful energies? Most of their energies are expended in study and, to a limited extent, in sports and in developing relationships

with peers of their own sex. Girls are more free in expressing affection for each other, such as holding hands while
walking, but almost never hug or kiss one another.

Only a few decades ago girls in middle school formed
so-called "s" relationships with "s" standing for sister,
between older and younger girls. Edward Norbeck noted
that Japanese middle school girls also formed "s" relationships.[1] To form such a relationship, a senior girl took the
initiative by asking a friend to introduce her to a freshman girl with whom she would like to have an "s" relationship. If the freshman girl agreed, they began the relationship. The younger girl addressed the older girl by the
term ŏnni (elder sister) but the older girl addressed the
younger by her personal name. Usually, the senior girl
first wrote letters and sent gifts to the younger girl. Such
exchanges furnished them much excitement. Their letters
were often filled with expressions of love and admiration
for one another, with a touch of romantic ferver. The "sisters" visited with one another in their homes or went on
picnics with groups of their friends who also had "s" relationships. Such a relationship provided an avenue for the
girls to channel their youthful romantic feelings. However,
the relationship did not involve any kind of sexual feelings or acts, as evident in a homosexual relationship in
the United States, but operated strictly on a platonic level.
Platonic relationships are much admired and romanticized
in Korea and in Japan, where open sexual expressions are
generally looked down upon with contempt.

Dating between the sexes is generally permitted after
graduation from high school. At this time girls are permitted to use make-up and face cream or powder, but in a
modest manner. They may change their hair style from
pigtails to permanent waves, and wear clothes of their

choice instead of the uniforms they wore throughout their school years. However, girls are careful not to expose their bodies, especially their arms, legs, bosoms and backs etc. If a girl exposes much of her body she is considered a loose woman. Only a few decades ago, girls who walked on the street wearing sleeveless blouses, which exposed their arms, were stopped by the police and chastised. However, some of this has greatly changed in recent years by the influx of Western fashion and by changing attitudes toward attire.

Even today, however, men and women do not freely interact with one another in a social gathering, and tend to interact mostly with members of the same sex. There are several reasons for this. First, since they were brought up with little socialization with the opposite sex, they feel uneasy in mixed social situations. Secondly, people think, for example, that if a woman relates to a man in a friendly manner, she has probably had much contact with men. This is considered undesirable. Popularity with the opposite sex gives one a negative reputation. While young men are condoned for having some sexual experiences before they marry, chastity is greatly emphasized for women before marriage. There are some indications, however, that today the number of young people living together unmarried is increasing in large cities. Yet pregnancy before and outside marriage still becomes a family calamity and a cause for social ostracism. Generally speaking, however, promiscuity is denounced on the ground of moral degeneration, as well as because of the danger of venereal disease. These social taboos and sanctions, along with the enforcement of segregation between the sexes from an early age, have largely eliminated much of sexual and dating problems as well as the sexual perversions and violence prevalent in the United States.

4
Methods of Discipline

In the course of raising children, parents in all cultures face disciplinary problems. Yet, each culture has its own methods of training and disciplining its children, in conformity with its societal values and goals.

Methods of discipline are primarily determined by the type of social structure of a given culture. Since the type of social structure of Confucian and American culture is different, the methods of discipline used in each culture are correspondingly different. In the United States, where the individual is the most basic social unit, individual rights and responsibilities are emphasized. Accordingly, American parents train their child to stand up for his own rights and the rights of others, to be autonomous, and to become independent of them. To bring up a child to be a unique individual, responsible for himself, is the ultimate goal of American parents.

In contrast, in Korea and other East Asian countries where the family is the basic social unit, the individual is primarily part of the family. Accordingly, Korean parents train their child not to think for himself but to think of himself as part of the group. They put greater emphasis on teaching their children to be loyal to their group—whether family or nation—than on individual rights or responsibilities. As a result, they tend to become easily aroused when they feel their group or nation is criticized, but not when the human rights of their fellow citizens are violated. The concept of "our-ness" rather than "my-ness" is emphasized. Korean children say "our mother" or "our family," instead of "my mother" or "my family." In school and at home the child is exhorted to obey authority and to conform to group norms and be like everyone else. Thus the value of uniformity and conformity is strongly instilled in children from an early age.

To bring up such a child, parents use strong authority, commanding, exhortation, fear-inspiring tactics or, as the last resort, physical punishment. Mothers use these methods in varying degrees, depending on the age of the child. During the preschool years, the mother tends to be excessively indulgent and often does not discipline her child, feeling he is too young to know better and that discipline is more appropriate for the older child. As a result, there are many spoiled children walking around, particularly in the preschool-age group. The mother's typical way of dealing with a crying child is to pacify him with some sweet or toy, or to command him to stop crying. Frequently, however, the mother or baby-sitting relatives use fear-inspiring tactics to control the child's behavior. For instance, the mother will take the crying child outside the house, pretend to give him away to a stranger, and command him to stop crying. The child will get frightened and scream, but the mother will not take him back inside until he stops crying.[1]

Similarly, if the mother does not want her child to go near the sea, she may warn him that a water vampire will pull him into the water. Or if she does not want him to go outside after dark, she may warn him that a begger will whisk him away. One adoptive mother said that in the beginning their 5-year-old boy whined and kicked a great deal. At one point she told him, "We don't do that here. Only a bad boy does that." He suddenly stopped whining and kicking. From what he related to her, she learned that the words "bad boy" reminded him of the intimidation the child-care worker in his orphanage often used: "If you are a bad boy, Jesus will come and whisk you away."

As the child reaches school-age, a Korean mother does not indulge him so much as she once did, but suddenly becomes strict with him. When the usual methods of discipline—commanding, exhortation and fear-inspiring tactics—do not work, the mother often resorts to physical punishment. Whipping with a twig or stick is the most common form of punishment, with the blows usually directed at the child's legs or back. Many adopted children, speaking about their past experiences, have told their American parents that they were whipped by their birth parents or relatives with a stick or a broom handle when they misbehaved or disobeyed. One 15-year-old girl who came here when she was 11 said, "I had a habit of talking back to my mom and would often blow up. My mom would whip me with a stick. I got all kinds of bruises and cuts on my legs. Then my mom felt sorry and put bandages over them."

Another popular method of disciplining older children is to inspire in them fear of public opinion or ridicule. If a mother does not want her child to do a certain thing, she will say, "If you do that, other people will say something about you or laugh at you." Such a method of discipline also tends to discourage a child from thinking and acting independently. At the same time the child learns to judge others or their behavior as "bad" or "good" in terms of its degree of conformity to the norms, rather than the principles involved. Furthermore, he becomes easily disposed to ridicule or laugh at those who do not conform to social norms or who are different in some way from those norms. One adoptive mother said of their 10-year-old son, "Whenever he sees any abnormal physical aspect of people, he breaks into fits of uncontrollable laughter. But, if other people laugh at him, he gets very serious and touchy." Obviously, this indicates that the methods of discipline and socialization used in a given culture are closely related to the type of personality it produces.

Compared to Korean methods of discipline, American methods are considerably different in character. The most outstanding characteristics of American methods are reasoning, asking, explaining, isolation or spanking. Unlike a Korean mother, an American mother is not so much concerned with public approval or ridicule, as with the principles involved in her child's behavior. She would say, "Do not worry about what other people say. Do what you think right for you." When her child misbehaves, the American mother first asks him why he did what he did, points out why she disapproves of his behavior, or explains why he cannot do certain things, rather than commanding, exhorting, scolding or intimidating. By these methods, the mother gives her child a chance to think about what he did, or to understand the reasons why she disapproves of his behavior. Such approaches tend to teach the child values based on principles rather than on social norms, as well as to help him develop his mind.

The majority of adoptive parents reported that they used reasoning as a prime method of disciplining a misbehaving child, often followed by isolating him in his room. One mother said, "If Jamie has done something we disapprove of, we usually spend time talking with him about his actions. Sometimes he might need a period of sitting by himself until he is ready to talk. We use isolation followed by discussion to solve most problems we encounter. We try to give lots of praise for positive behavior."

However, many parents found that in the beginning reasoning did not work too well with the child. This is largely because the child had a language barrier and also had never been disciplined by reasoning. In addition, at this time the child undergoes a tremendous amount of frustration, anxiety and confusion, due to the change of culture and environment, which he often expresses in temper tantrums. In dealing with such a child, parents often resorted to spanking him, then isolating him in his room until he stopped crying or gained some perspective on his behavior. One mother said of their 5-year-old boy, "In the beginning, he sat and whined a great deal. We tried to reason with him, but words didn't work with him. So we spanked him and sent him to his room and let him stay there for awhile. Then we would go in and ask him why he was sent there. We didn't really want to spank him, because we have rarely done so with our other children." Another mother said, "I don't believe in spanking children. But Tom can be very mischievous or naughty, so his father will sometimes spank him. When this happens, Tom says, "I wish a different family had picked me out."

Another popular method of American discipline is giving rewards for positive behavior or taking away privileges for negative behavior. One mother of a 9-year-old boy said, "Steve has a bad habit of taking off his clothes and dropping them on the floor. I always tell him he must pick up his clothes and must put his shoes away neatly. Unless he does these things, he doesn't get what he wants. He loves to have me tickle his back and also wants me to read him a story at bedtime. So, for the most part, he is willing to cooperate because he wants these things."

For older children, privileges often mean the freedom to go out and do things they enjoy. Parents often take such a privilege away from the child as punishment. One 19-year-old girl who came here at age 12 said, "Whenever I didn't do things my mom asked me to do, I was grounded. One day I dried clothes, leaving them in the dryer. Then I went over to my girl friend's place. My mom came home and got upset and grounded me for two weeks."

5
Personality

Personality is made of two large components, one influenced by the over-all culture in which a person has developed and the other by his individual attributes, such as circumstances and heredity. The personality component discussed in this chapter is mainly that formed by the forces of culture.

Anthropologist Ralph Linton terms the culture-bound component of personality as "the basic personality type": "The basic personality type for any society is that personality configuration which is shared by the bulk of the society's members as a result of the early experiences which they have in common. It does not correspond to the total personality of the individual but rather to the projective systems or, in different phraseology, the value-attitude systems which are basic to the individual's personality configuration. Thus the same basic personality type may be reflected in many different forms of behavior and may enter into many different total personality configurations."[1]

The basic personality type for any culture group is shaped by the type of social structure, child care system, and other cultural factors commonly shared by that group. For this reason, the basic personality type of one culture group, as opposed to another, should be understood in the light of these factors. Ralph Linton writes, "This brings us at once to the field of acculturation studies, an area in which the concept of basic personality types may prove of paramount importance."[2] This is indeed true, and it directly applies to the situation where two or more culture groups are thrown together in a family relationship, as in the case of Oriental children in American homes. With this in mind, this chapter will discuss some of the child's personality traits that parents found most contrasting to their own. Yet, this study indicates that the longer children live in American homes the more they acquire American personality traits and lose the traits they acquired in their previous culture.

Obedient or Demanding

Many adoptive parents described their children's behavior as characteristically respectful, obedient, polite, clean, neat, orderly, controlled etc. These traits are clearly the by-products of Confucian authoritarian culture, as well as other cultural and social conditions. For instance, the traits of neatness and cleanliness are strongly desired and required from a practical point of view. Because Koreans, like Japanese, sit and sleep on the floor of a room, the rooms need to be kept as neat and clean as possible. While some parents were pleased with these traits, others expressed some concern, depending on their preference as well as the degree of such traits exhibited by the child. One mother described their 7-year-old girl whom they adopted at age 5. "When she first came, she was very neat and kept her room immaculate. She would stack up her socks in the same direction. But she's totally out of this now. If I let her, she would leave her room in a total mess." Quite a few parents seemed to attribute the child's neatness or cleanliness to her institutionalized life. Although that life may reinforce such a trait to the extreme, these traits are found as often among children who have lived with their birth mothers or relatives.

As already discussed, in the Confucian culture the child is subjected to strong parental authority. As a result, the child learns to be submissive and obedient to authority, but also learns to be demanding from his authoritarian parents. The tendency to demand often surfaces in the form of *ŏrigang,* a behavior which can be defined as a begging or demanding to be indulged, when a child wants something from his mother. Psychodynamically speaking, *ŏrigang* is an interesting behavior and deserves some discussion here. It is the child's way of responding or relating to an authoritarian and indulging mother, when he wants something from her. *Ŏrigang* is most commonly observable among younger children (although also in older children) because they are more indulged by their mothers. The behavior of *ŏrigang* is also found in adults, particularly in a younger sibling when he wants something from his elder sibling.

Interesting enough, Japanese psychiatrist Takeo Doi noted a similar behavior among Japanese children in the form of *amae.* The meaning of the Japanese word *amae* corresponds to that of the Korean word *ŏrigang.* The verb form of *amae* is *amaeru*. Doi writes, "Amaeru can be translated 'to depend and presume on another's love,' (or) 'to seek and bask in another's indulgence.' "[3] There is no English word corresponding to either *ŏrigang* or *amaeru*, simply because an American child does not behave *ŏrigang* or *amaeru*. He does not behave so because he has been brought up to be independent and self-reliant, usually by a mother who is neither indulgent nor demanding. One perceptive mother observed that their 8-year-old adoptee, who had lived with her birth mother prior to her coming to the United States, did a great deal of "begging whine" in the beginning. The mother said, "When she begs, I ask her, 'Please don't tease Mommy,' and then she grins and stops her begging."

On the other hand, children who had no maternal care when young or lived in an orphanage for a long period of time may not behave *ŏrigang* because their environment did not provide them with an indulging mother but only authoritarian adults. As a result, these children often become emotionally independent.

As the child gets older and is no longer much indulged, he gives up the behavior of *ŏrigang* as part of the growing-up process. However, the child may express his emotion of *ŏrigang* in the form of demanding, when he wants something from his parents. One American father who adopted a 12-year-old girl said, "We had planned to buy certain things for her, but she would jump ahead of us before we were ready. When we bought something for her, it was more a way of meeting her demands than doing something for her on our own." The father's feeling about the child's behavior is equally a by-product of his American upbringing, in which he learned to ask his parents when he wanted something or wait until they were ready to buy things for him on their own. However, the girl had only learned to beg or demand when she wanted something from her mother. In this case, there is another dimension of the girl's behavior to be understood. The girl said, "There was a rumor in Korea that American people are rich. I remember people telling me that my American parents will give me everything I wanted. So I expected they would buy anything I asked for." The girl's account is easily believable because many Koreans assume from watching glamorous Hollywood movies that most Americans are "rich."

Being Unexpressive or Unresponsive

Many parents felt that one of the most difficult problems they had to deal with during the initial months was the child's inability to express and respond to them. One mother who adopted an 11-year-old girl said, "Susan does have respect for authority, older people and parents. Even though she was very angry, it was her duty to be proper and respectful and to hold her feelings back. Even when she was able to speak some English, she held all her feelings in and sat in silence. She wouldn't explain to us why she was crying or angry or what her feelings were. That was really frustrating to us." Another mother who adopted a 9-year-old boy who is now 17 said, "When you ask him about something, you never get the full answer. His answer is either 'yes' or 'no' without a detail. Sometimes he doesn't give the straight answer to a legitimate question like 'Did you put your coat downstairs?' Because his answer is noncommital, communication is difficult. You get frustrated and feel uptight about this, because you never know what he's thinking and you often have to figure out what his right answer might be."

Moreover, American mothers have been taught to believe that interpersonal problems can be solved by a give-and-take communication between the persons involved. So they encourage their children to express their feelings. A mother said of their 10-year-old boy, whom they adopted at age 7, "He is a child who doesn't always express his feelings in words. We have tried to draw his feelings out—good and bad—by giving him time to express verbally what he is feeling. It has taken quite a bit of patience on our part to wait until he was ready to speak. It has taken a lot of holding and touching also. He is doing a better job of expressing how he feels, but this is still an area we will constantly have to work with."

The frustrations of these mothers is understandable because they are accustomed to children who are expressive and responsive. Of course, part of each child's difficulties in expressing himself was related to his language barrier. But also, he had been brought up under a system of child care that had trained him to suppress his emotions—whether joy or anger. In Confucian culture, an expression of emotions is discouraged because it is thought to disrupt proper relationships between superiors and inferiors. As a result, if a child does not wish to get into trouble with his parents or other superiors, he chooses to remain quiet and unresponsive. Some of the children may use their conditioned unresponsiveness as passive defiance against their superiors. Such a defense mechanism might work relatively well with Confucian parents who expect their child to be unresponsive, but it may frustrate American parents who expect the opposite. One mother who adopted a 13-year-old girl said, "I ask her questions, but she doesn't say either "yes" or "no.""

Absolute silence. This drives me up to the wall. This is the most difficult problem I have to cope with." Another mother suggested a similar difficulty she had with their 8-year-old girl: "What I noticed especially was that at least once a day she became extremely stubborn. She seemed to pull a mask down over her face and refused to look at anyone."

The child's inability to express or respond is largely a by-product of a strict parent-child relationship in which the parents demand obedience from the child but do not permit a great deal of give-and-take communication with him. If there is communication it is usually one-way from parent to child. Parents are not so much interested in understanding the child as in instructing and exhorting him. In fact, in the authority-obedience oriented parent-child relationship two-way communication is neither important nor desired. Parents and child may be in each other's company a great deal, but they do not exchange thoughts or emotions as American parents and their children do. For instance, a Korean mother does not greet her child with "good morning" or "good night" or "hello." She is more concerned with her child's physical needs than his emotional needs. A 16-year-old girl who came here at age 11 said, "My Korean Mom didn't talk very much to me, except for warnings like, 'Be careful when you go outside,' or asking 'Are you hungry?'" When a mother offers her child food or clothes, she rarely asks his preference, but gives him whatever she thinks he should have. Such child care does not give the child many opportunities to think for himself or make decisions on his own.

This is in direct contrast to the American parent-child relationship. Communication—sharing experiences, ideas and feelings—is at the heart of American living. Although American parents and their children are often engaged in their own activities and do not spend a great deal of time together, when they are together they communicate with one another a great deal by smiling, greeting or chatting. One adoptive mother said of their 17-year-old boy whom they adopted at age 9, "Peter doesn't ask many questions or say much. He doesn't share his experiences with others in the family. For instance, if he wins something he's quiet about it, until one of us notices and asks about it. If my American-born children win something, they get excited, run home and say, 'Mom! Look what I got!'"

In the United States the free exchange of experiences or emotions is more possible because American culture puts strong emphasis on sharing experiences with one another. This emphasis has risen from the fact that American social structure is organized on the basis of equality and individualism. While equality permits individuals to relate to one another more easily, individualism is geared to strengthen the mental or emotional well-being of the individual, largely achieved by communication with others. On the basis of these assumptions, an American mother tends to communicate with her child a great deal by smiling, hugging or talking. She greets the child with "good morning" or "good night" or "hello." When she offers breakfast, she asks the child what kind of cereals he would like or how his eggs should be cooked, etc. When she sends the child to school, she hugs or kisses him and says, "Have a good day!" When the child returns home, she greets, "Did you have a good day?" If the mother goes out, she tells her child where she is going and when she plans to return; the child is expected to do the same.

Even when family members are not together, they know where the others are and can reach one another in case they need to do so. In this way they can safeguard each other.

Quite a few parents reported that their adopted child had the habit of running off in stores or supermarkets or leaving the house without telling them where he was going. This lack of communication created some problems. A mother, who had some serious problems with their teenage daughter, complained "When she went out, she would just take off without telling where or with whom she was going and what she was going to do. We trusted her but as parents we're responsible for her and had the right to know these things. But she didn't think it was necessary to tell us."

Another custom related to communication is that of expressing appreciation or apology. Here in the United States hardly a day goes by without our saying "thank-you" to someone. Family members frequently express appreciation or apology to one another—parents to their children or vice versa. However, in Confucian culture, an expression of thanks is generally reserved for those outside the family—usually when an inferior thanks a superior for a favor. As a rule, social superiors rarely say "thank-you," "I'm sorry," or "please" to their inferior—children or servants—largely because they are superior to them and take them for granted. By the same token, parents do not say these things to their child or children to their parents. One American mother related an instance in which she thanked her 12-year-old daughter for setting the dinner table. The girl said, "We are family. You don't have to say 'thank-you.'" Another mother commented about her 17-year-old boy, "He never apologizes for anything or says 'thank-you.' Once, when I bought something for him, he put it away quietly without saying anything. Then he came back after a while and said, 'thank-you.' That was the first time he ever said it. Oh, I was so happy! I still remember it."

Dependent or Independent

In Confucian culture where a child is not viewed as an autonomous being, parents demand unconditional obedience from him, and at the same time decide things for him and do things for him rather than helping him do things for himself. In contrast, the value of independence and self-reliance is strongly emphasized in American culture. American parents try to bring up a child to be independent at an early age by teaching him to think for himself and do things or solve problems on his own. One mother explains, "We strongly stress independence, so that when he is 18 he can cope with his problems." Conditioned to such value-attitudes, an American mother teaches a 2-year-old child how to hold a spoon or how to button his shirt as soon as he is physically and mentally capable of doing so.

When American parents found their adopted child had a strong tendency to depend on them, they tried to teach him to be self-reliant. One mother who adopted two girls and a 5-year-old boy said, "A week or so after his arrival, we stopped waiting on him, dressing him, feeding him, picking up his clothes, making his bed etc. We showed his 3-year-old sister how to help him with these chores. He cooperated and tried to do things for himself. Occasionally, during the next couple of years, he decided he couldn't do something for himself, or wouldn't try.

Our approach is: "Never do for a child what he can do for himself. For instance, if he couldn't get his coat buttoned, boots on, etc. (after managing this for months), he simply did not go with the rest of the family or out to play, wherever he wanted to go—until he was dressed. We expected as much from him at age five as his 3-year-old sister could accomplish, and he responded. He was emotionally dependent for a matter of months, during which we tried to give him a great deal of love and support and make sure he was not left alone in a strange environment. Gradually he began to see we would not leave him and not return; he had to go places alone (Sunday school, etc.) and become independent."

However, the mother found it was more difficult to teach the value of independence to their teenage girl, whom they adopted at age 16. The mother described the girl as: ". . . dependent and unable to do anything for herself, either physically or mentally. We have spent a great deal of time and thought on helping her to be independent and self-reliant. She is progressing. We have told her she is responsible for herself, for getting places on time and doing her school work, for remembering necessary items, her money, her clothes, her room, etc. Wrong or right, she makes her own decisions and if they are wrong, she suffers the consequences. For example, she decides she doesn't want to sing in special concert with the school choir on a Sunday afternoon so she stays home. She is the one who is bawled out by the choir director on Monday and it is her school grade that is lowered."

On the other hand, the girl had enormous problems to cope with because of the change of culture and language at her age. It appears that as an only child she was greatly pampered by her birth mother, usually the case for an only child. Her mother waited on her and did everything for her. As a result, she didn't learn to do things for herself or make decisions on her own. Now in her American home she is suddenly expected to do things for herself, in addition to having to cope with new language and new culture, which is the antithesis of the one she used to know.

One 15-year-old girl summed up the problems of adjusting to the American way of life, "My Korean mother made all decisions for me. But my American mother tried to make me decide on things, like choosing my own clothes. I had a hard time making decisions. I find the American ways very difficult." Another child, a 15-year-old boy who came here at age 10, expressed a similar view: "My Korean Mom was very protective of me. She tried to do everything for me. My American Mom tries to help me think and do on my own. She expects me to do things by myself. I still feel more comfortable being part of a group than being independent. I'm not ready to go out and do things on my own."

By doing things for him, the Korean mother satisfies her child's dependency needs effortlessly but impedes the development of his ability to think for himself and fosters his dependency on her. On the other hand, dependency thus fostered does not affect him in achieving success in his adult life in Korea, as it might in the United States, because success does not depend so much on independence as on knowing whose authority to depend on and obey. Strong emphasis on the maintenance of the status quo has cancelled out the advancement of society.

According to a few parents, while their children were disposed to dependency in task-oriented areas, they showed emotional independence in certain situations. One mother said of their 7-year-old girl who had been with them for one year, "Once, when she missed her school bus, Diane walked to school alone and didn't mind it at all. While she is quite self-sufficient in this way, she easily gets lost in a social situation." A similar example was given by a mother of two sisters, who said, "Often when we go out in the evening we leave them alone, knowing that they can take care of themselves. They are mature and independent in this way, but immature and dependent in other areas." Their emotional independence seems to tie in with their early upbringing, in which they had little communication with their parents and, by American standards, experienced considerable emotional isolation.

The Tendency to Interfere

Another trait closely related to authoritarian culture is a tendency to give unrequested advice or to interfere in others' affairs. Koreans and other East Asians have a strong tendency to do this, because they have been so taught by their authoritarian parents. This tendency is born out of the Confucian family system which stresses group rights and responsibilities over those of the individual. People are taught to feel responsible for everyone whom they consider "one of us," and exhorted on the virtue of helping others. This conditioning often leads to a tendency of advice-giving and interference in others' affairs, without being asked. Psychodynamically speaking, this tendency is also motivated by the desire to dominate. For example, when a person takes the liberty of telling his relatives what to do about their parents or children without being asked, he does so without any concern about hurting their feelings.

The child brought up in Confucian culture learns this

tendency to interfere from his parents and other adults. Quite a few American parents noted that their adopted children often intruded in affairs that did not concern them directly. One mother said their 6-year-old girl liked to mediate quarrels between other children, with her command, "Do not fight!" Another mother described their 7-year-old boy as a "busy-body" who got himself into things that did not concern him. If she asked her daughter to get something for her, the boy would jump up and get it himself. She said that once, when a neighbor informed her that someone had parked a car in their parking place, their son stepped in and said, "He shouldn't have parked there." If he thought his mother did things in the wrong way, he would say, "That's not the way to do it."

In contrast, an American child tends to mind his own business and does not concern himself with others' affairs because he is brought up to respect his own rights and those of others. He is brought up to think for himself, to be responsible for himself, and to defend himself against bullies, if necessary. He is also expected to be self-sufficient within the limits of his capacity at a given stage of development. But, if a teenage boy faces a problem beyond his ability, he is expected to take the initiative and discuss it with his parents or ask help from them.

Accustomed to such notions and ways, an American father had been hesitant to correct their 16-year-old daughter with her English, for fear he might hurt her feelings. However, it is quite probable that the girl had been expecting her parents to take the initiative in correcting her mistakes, without her asking them to do so. In the past her Korean mother or teachers had corrected any mistakes she made, without her asking them to do so. Koreans tend to be more concerned that the child does not make mistakes than that they might hurt his feelings by correcting him. The American father said to the girl, "Here in America we do not correct others' mistakes outright. It's impolite to do so. From now on, do you want us to correct your English?" The girl nodded her head vigorously, as if she had been expecting it all along.

Obsession with Money

Money is probably the most important commodity needed if men are to survive in society. Yet money can mean a great deal more to one culture group than to another, depending on the type of society in which it lives. If a society is based on an ethical system which concerns itself exclusively with man's physical reality, as in Confucianism, and not so much with man's spiritual reality, as in Christianity, it tends to foster in man a strong obsession with money and material things.

As a result, children who were brought up in Confucian culture tend to value material things far more than the spiritual. Not surprisingly, many parents reported that their adopted children showed an inordinate interest in money and material things (car, house, clothes, etc.), as well as strong status-consciousness. Their most frequently used phrases were "lots of money," "rich," or "high class." One mother said that their 10-year-old boy always picked out the most expensive items—toys, or clothes or sports equipment—and flaunted them before his friends. Some parents expressed concern over the child's obsession with material things or status, and wondered how they could teach him spiritual values such as kindness, consideration, generosity, or respect for others' feelings or rights.

Also frequently reported was the child's tendency to hoard money. This trait is no doubt also culturally fostered. In the Confucian culture one of the most stressed virtues is frugality. One mother who adopted a 11-year-old girl said they had given a one-dollar allowance each week for a year. At the end of the year they learned to their surprise that she had saved most of it. Asked why she had done so, she replied she wanted to become "rich." The mother told her she could not become rich on her allowance. The girl's explanation was: "Money meant so much to me while I was in Korea and also when I first came here. As soon as my parents gave me an allowance, I saved most of it, because while I was in Korea I had learned that saving money was a good thing. I still remember a story I read in a comic book about a kid who saved all his money and gave it to his mother. When you read about such a character, you try to be like that person. So I tried to save the allowance my parents gave me. I told my girlfriend I was saving money to make a trip to Korea. I was young and thought that's what I wanted to do. But this got to my parents; they got very upset."

On the other hand, the child's tendency to hoard money may also be related to his experience of extreme poverty. Many children adopted by American couples have lived in abject poverty over which they had no control. To them money is precious. Jacky, a 7-year-old girl who came from a fatherless family, hoarded her money and possessions. Her mother said, "Jacky started to receive 25 cents each week for her allowance as soon as she arrived. She kept this money, and other money she received as a gift in various hiding places. She loves to count her money, and wouldn't spend any money for a long time. Some of her birthday gifts are still laid out under her bed—not to be used by herself or anyone else."

6
Language

Historical Background

For centuries, Koreans and Japanese used Chinese characters as the essential part of their language. Then, in the mid-15th century, a group of Korean scholars working under the auspices of King *Sejong* invented the Korean phonetic system, which is commonly known as *hangŭl*. Thus, the present-day Korean language consists of two parts, Chinese characters and *hangŭl*. While *hangŭl* is exclusively based on syllabic symbols, Chinese characters are based on pictorial symbols of the objects of everyday life. Because of the pictorial quality of Chinese characters, Koreans, Japanese and Chinese can communicate with one another through written Chinese characters. However, they may not be able to understand one another through their spoken language, because they have their native phonetic system by which Chinese characters are pronounced.

Even after Koreans invented their syllabic symbols, they have continuely used Chinese characters for convenience, out of habit, and also for pedantry or fashion. This is also true with the Japanese. Traditionally, and perhaps even now, persons who can write Chinese characters are considered to be cultured or scholarly. However, Koreans today do not use Chinese characters as much as they once did; since they gained their independence from the Japanese at the end of World War II, their government has been urging them to use *hangŭl*. This urging is intended not only to promote their native tongue and linguistic independence, but also because, for the vast majority of the people, Chinese characters are extremely difficult to learn. Although a majority of the older generations still use Chinese characters along with *hangŭl*, the younger generations use *hangŭl* exclusively. Whether or not Chinese characters are used, their influence on *hangŭl* remains, because many *hangŭl* words used today have been derived from the phonetic sounds with which Chinese characters are pronounced.

Phonetic System

The Korean phonetic system consists of nineteen consonants and twenty-one vowels and diphthongs. However, the system does not have certain English sounds, such as /r/, /l/, /v/, /f/, or /th/. For this reason, most Koreans find it extremely difficult to pronounce these English sounds. It is also true that certain Korean sounds do not have English equivalents.

According to many parents and teachers interviewed, Korean-born children had trouble producing the sounds of these English letters or pronouncing words that have any of these sounds. To begin with, the child often distorted the /r/ sound to one approaching a /w/ sound.

Examples are: The word "rabbit" is pronounced as "wabbit," the word "right" as "wite" or the word "read" as "wead," etc.

Occasionally, some children left out the /r/ sound altogether, especially when it comes in the body of a word. For example, "everybody," is pronounced as "evvabody." In addition, they often confused the /r/ and /l/ sounds and produced the /l/ sound instead of the /r/ sound or vice versa. Some children also had difficulty pronouncing words that have the blends /cr/, /br/, /cl/, /bl/, /dl/ or words that have /r/ and /l/ sounds, like "children."

The child often pronounced the /f/ sound as a /p/ sound. Examples: "Five" is pronounced as "pive."

"Four" is pronounced as "pour."

"Elephant" is pronounced as "elepant."

The child often pronounced the /th/ sound as /d/ or /t/. Examples: "Thank you" is pronounced as "tank you."

"Fifth" is pronounced as "pit."

"This" is pronounced as "dis."

"Then" is pronounced as "den."

"That" is pronounced as "dat."

"There" is pronounced as "dare."

"Them" is pronounced as "dem."

Other sounds the child had trouble producing are those vowel sounds: /e/, /i/, /o/ /u/. One mother, reported that their 8-year-old child pronounced "stupa" for "stupid." The English phonic sound /ĭ/ may be especially difficult for some children to produce, because the Korean syllabic system does not have a sound approaching it, although it has a sound approaching the English phonic sound /ē/. As a result, they may likely produce /ē/ sound for /ĭ/ sound or may skip the /ĭ/ sound altogether.

Sentence Structure

In the Korean sentence as in the English, the subject comes at the beginning of a sentence. However, the word order in the predicate is completely the reverse of that of the English sentence, with an object preceding a verb.[1]

Example: I go to school.

Na nŭn   hakkyo   e   kanda.
(I)   (school) (to) (go)

In the above Korean sentence there is no preposition before the noun "*hakkyo*", but it is followed by a post-positional particle "*e.*" In a way the post-positional particle "*e*" serves the same function as the English preposition "to" in indicating a noun's case.

In line with the reversed position of object-verb in a Korean sentence, a relative clause precedes a head noun, which it modifies.

Example: I like my aunt who lives in New York.

Nyu Yok e sanŭn naŭi ajŏmŏni rŭl nanŭn johananda.

(New York) (live) (my)   (aunt)   (I)   (like).

Another distinct difference between English and Korean sentences is that, in the interrogative case, the Korean sentence does not change the position of subject and verb, as in English. The interrogative case in Korean sentence is indicated merely by placing an affix, /ka/, /ni/, or /nya/ right after the verb at the end of the sentence. Which one of the interrogative forms is to be used is mainly dependent on who is speaking to whom, that is, whether to one's superior or inferior. For instance, if a mother is addressing her child, she may use the affix /ni/ or /nya/. If a child is speaking to his mother, he may use the affix /ka/.

Example A: Did you go to school? (Mother asks her child.)

Hakkyo   e   katsŏt-ni.
(school) (to) (went) (?)

Example B: Did you go to school? (Child asks her mother.)

Hakkyo   e   katsŭmni-ka.
(school) (to) (went)   (?)

In view of these basic differences between the two languages, when the child arrives here he is likely to make some "mother-tongue-interference" errors in his English sentence, because he still thinks in the structural pattern of the Korean language. Many parents and teachers reported that in the beginning the child reversed the word order of verb-object in English, like "I school go" or "Mom, Paul my school come." Also, the child often left out a preposition before a noun, as in "I go school." A few parents also observed that the child did not change the word order of subject-verb in the interrogative case, as in "What time it is?" or "How old he is?"

Personal Pronouns

In the Korean sentence personal pronouns do not play an important role. It is not always essential to indicate personal pronouns, such as "I," "me," or "my." For instance, Koreans do not say "my head aches" or "my stomach hurts" but just say "head aches" or "stomach hurts." Also, subjective pronouns, "I" or "you," are often left out of a sentence, as in the following example.

> *Father asks.*   *Son replies.*
> Did you go to school?   Yes, I went.

(Nŏ) Hakkyo e katawat-ni. Ne, (jŏ) katawatsŭmnida.
(You) (school) (to) (went) (?) (Yes, sir) (I) (went.)

In the above father's question and son's reply, the subjective pronouns "*nŏ*" (you) and "*jŏ*" (I) are left out in the Korean sentences. Koreans may say that since the father and son are speaking to one another and no one else, it is not necessary for them to indicate "you" or "I" in their sentences. However, the omission of personal pronouns often contributes to the lack of clarity in communication as to who-did-what or who-did-what-to-whom. It also diminishes the individual's sense of himself.

The omission of personal pronouns may well be related to psychological conditionings to which Koreans have been subjected by their culture. In the Confucian culture a person is discouraged from having a strong sense of "I-ness," independent of his family or group. Since in this culture a person is primarily part of a group, whether family, village or nation, his identity is first and foremost defined by his relationship to his group, rather than by his own person or self. For example, when an adult meets a child, he often asks him his father's name instead of his own name. Acquaintances identify a person as the son of so-and-so or the younger brother of so-and-so or the elder sister of so-and-so, rather than by his or her personal name. Needless to say, this custom of identification weakens one's sense of individual identification but strengthens that of group identification.

While personal pronouns are often omitted, as in the above examples, there are occasions in which they must be indicated. For example, if a father asks his son, "Who opened the window?" Then, the son should reply, "I did," or "I did not," whichever the case may be. But he should express "I" in the humble form, which is "*jŏ*," because he is addressing a superior.

In the Korean language there are roughly three levels of indicating first person pronoun "I": the humble form, "*jŏ*," which is used when one is speaking to a superior; the common form, "*nae*," which is used when one is speaking to his equals or strangers, and the respectful form, which is usually expressed by the relational noun or title of a person, like "the father" or "the company president." Which pronoun is to be used in a given sentence is largely determined by who is speaking to whom. When a father is speaking to his son, he refers to himself as "the father," the respectful form of "I." If a son is speaking to his father (superior), he refers to himself as "*jŏ*," the humbling form of "I." Between equals or strangers, one refers to himself as "*nae*," the common form of "I."

By the same token, there are roughly three levels to indicate the second person pronoun "you." The common form, "*tangsin*," is used if one is speaking to his equals or strangers. The demeaning or familiar form, "*nŏ*," is used if one is speaking to an inferior or a close friend. The respectful form is expressed by a relational noun such as "the father" or a title plus family name, such as "Dr. Kim," etc. Which of the three forms should be used is, again, largely determined by who is speaking to whom. For example, when a father (superior) is speaking to his son (inferior), he refers to his son as "*nŏ*," the demeaning form of "you." However, when a son is speaking to his father, he refers to his father as "the father," a respectful form of "you." If speaking to a stranger, the speaker refers to him as "*tangsin*."

Koreans prefer to identify themselves by a relational noun or a title plus family name rather than by a personal name, because the former is more respectful. For instance, married persons prefer to identify themselves or be identified by others by their relational noun, as "the father of so-and-so" or "the mother of so-and-so" rather than by their personal names. For this reason, a personal name, particularly that of an adult woman, is often not known by her family or outsiders. Often a child may not know his mother's name or a person may not know the name of her sister-in-law. However, the name of an adult man, usually the head of a family, is well known in his family or to outsiders, because his name is often mentioned in identifying his wife, his children, or others in the family.

Furthermore, when a child addresses unrelated adults, friends of his parents or neighbors, he never addresses them by their first names, for doing so is considered extremely rude. Instead, he addresses them by a relational noun, like "uncle," "aunt," "grandmother" or "grandfather," depending on their age or sex. In general social situations outside the family, one refers to the other person by his family name plus a title, Dr., Mr., Miss, or Mrs. or "the teacher" (a polite term used for someone who is one's senior in age or position.) Likewise, Koreans refer to their President as "Excellency" plus "the President" in either his presence or absence, rarely by his personal name or a personal pronoun, such as "he" or "you." Doing so is tantamount to insult, because the second or third person pronoun "you" or "he" is used only in addressing or referring to one's equal or strangers. Like Koreans, Japanese also refer to their Emperor as "Highness" plus "the Emperor," never by his name or a personal pronoun such as "he" or "you." Japanese and

Koreans, who are highly status-conscious, can not imagine themselves addressing their Emperor or President (their superior) as "you" or to be addressed by their servant (their inferior) as "you," because it is less respectful. To know your superior and inferior and address them accordingly is regarded as a sign of high culture and erudition. This notion is largely inherited from the Confucian teachings which emphasize the maintenance of proper relations among people and stress that the proper addressing of people is an important part of maintaining such relationships.

Needless to say, the excessive emphasis on one's title or relational noun accounts for the tenuous role personal pronouns play in the Korean language. This is why personal pronouns are often omitted in a sentence. The child who is conditioned to such a language is likely to have some problems handling personal pronouns in the English language. Many parents and teachers reported that the child often left out personal (or impersonal) pronouns in all cases.

For example: (We) caught one then we let it go.

Tie (my) shoes.

He put (it) on the table.

Also, quite a few parents reported that when their child first arrived, he began sentences with "me" instead of "I." He would say, "Me happy," or "Me go school." Also, in the negative case the child used "no," in place of "do not" or "am not," as in "Me no happy," or "Me no eat."

Verb

The function of Korean verbs is significantly different

from that of English verbs in many respects. Most significantly, a Korean verb comes at the end of a sentence. Strictly speaking, a Korean verb has two parts—verb and verb-suffix—which are conjugated together. The verb-suffix is liable to change its form, depending on the verb's tense, as well as its affirmative, negative or interrogative case.

Example for present tense and affirmative case:

> I go to school.
> *Na nŭn hakkyo e kanda.*
> (I) (school) (to) (go)

Example for past tense:

> Yesterday I went to school.
> *Ŏje na nŭn hakkyo e kadda.*
> (yesterday) (I) (school) (went)

Example for future tense:

> Tomorrow I will go to school.
> *Naeil na nŭn hakkyo e kalkŏtsida.*
> (tomorrow) (I) (school) (will go)

Example for negative case, indicated by placing the affix "*an*" or "*mot*" before the verb "*kanda*" (go).

> I do not go to school.
> *Na nŭn hakkyo e an-kanda.*
> (I) (school) (do not go)

Furthermore, Korean verbs, for example, "*malhada*" (speak) do not change in terms of plurality or singularity, grammatical gender, or the first, second, third person case of subject. This greatly simplifies grammatical problems, but greatly contributes to lack of precision.

In view of these aspects of Korean verb, the child

learning to speak or write English is expected to have some problems handling English verbs. According to many parents and teachers, one of the most common errors the child made was failing to make agreement between subject and verb. For example, "Mom make a soup," or "She sit on a bed."

Of all the characteristics of the Korean verb, probably the most outstanding is that it changes its form in terms of who is speaking to whom. This function is totally alien to that of English verbs. For instance, if one is addressing a superior, one uses the respectful form of the verb-suffix. If one is addressing an inferior, one uses the humble form of the verb-suffix. The following examples clarify this point.

Example: Father speaks to his older son.

A. Did you give some money to your younger brother?

Nŏ ŭi   tongsaeng   ege   ton   ŭl juŏt-ni.

(your) (younger brother)   (money) (gave) (?)

B. Did you give some money to your mother?

Nŏ ŭi ŏmŏni ege ton ŭl tŭryŏt-ni.

(your mother) (money) (gave) (?)

In the above Korean sentences, one notes that the form of the verb (gave) is different in each sentence. In the "A" sentence where the father is referring to the younger son, he uses the demeaning form of the verb *"juŏt"* (gave), because he is inferior to the older son. In the "B" sentence, where the father is referring to the mother, he uses the respectful form of the verb *"tŭryŏt"* (gave), because she is superior to the son.

As in the above examples, the respectful form of verbs almost always tends to be multi-syllabic and longer than the humble form. As a result, the more polite and formal the speech or writings the more they contain multi-syllabic verbs which necessarily make the sentences long and wordy. The imperative of formality cancels out the speed and effectiveness of communication. In contrast, English verbs do not change in terms of the status of a person one is speaking or referring to. What is most stressed in the English language is clarity of meaning and brevity of expression. English teachers often exhort students: "Never use a long word (or sentence) when a short one would do."

No doubt, this status-function of Korean verbs makes the Korean language most difficult to learn, especially for English speaking people. Before deciding which form of a verb is appropriate in a given sentence, one has to know who is superior to whom. Those who have not lived in Korean society for long enough or as a member of a Korean family, would have no way of knowing by what standards one decides the superiority or inferiority of the other person.

Gender or Impersonal Pronouns

Korean language does not have grammatical gender (masculine or feminine) or impersonal pronouns (it, its). For instance, when one is referring to a particular man or woman in subjective and objective cases, one indicates "the man" or "the woman." In the possessive case one indicates "the man's" or "the woman's."

Many parents and teachers reported that the child showed some confusion over which gender pronoun to use. For example: the child would say, "*He* has two children," instead of "*She* has two children." He would say, "My sister didn't like *her*," instead of "My sister didn't like *him*." Or he would say, "What is *her* name?" instead of "what is *his* name?"

Plurality or Singularity

In the Korean language nouns are not pluralized.

> Example: My mother has apples.
> *Na ŭi ŏmŏni* nŭn *sagwa* rŭl *kajida.*
> (My) (mother)   (apple)   (has)

Needless to say, lack of plurality or singularity greatly contributes to ambiguity of communication; no one can know if a person has one or more than one apple, or apples of a particular kind. In comparison, in the English language this fact is always clarified by the use of singular or plural forms of the noun or by the modifier, "a," "the," "these," or "some," etc.

However, if the indication of a number of apples is required in a Korean sentence, one indicates it by adding a numeral adjective, such as "one," "two," "three" or "many" before the noun.

> Example: My mother has two apples.
> *Na ŭi ŏmŏni nŭn tuge ŭi sagwa* rŭl *kajida.*
> (My) (mother)   (two)   (apple)   (has)

Because of these characteristics of the Korean language, the child learning to speak English is bound to have some difficulty handling plurality or singularity. According to parents and teachers, one of the most common errors the child made was his failure to make a noun plural in either reading or writing.

Example: She has two book(s).
    Two girl(s) went to store.
    The boy(s) were playing.

In addition, the child also had trouble learning the irregular form of a plural noun. For example, he would say, "You can hear wolf howling," instead of "You can hear wolves howling."

Articles (definite or indefinite)

The Korean language does not have articles, either definite or indefinite.

Examples: I place a book on the desk.
    Na nŭn   chaeksan   ue chaek ŭl nohta.
    (I)   (desk)   (on) (book)   (place)

In the above Korean sentence, there is neither indefinite article before "book" nor definite article before "desk." Since the Korean language does not have articles, Koreans would say "book" or "desk," without being more specific. However, if it is necessary to indicate a particular book or desk, this can be indicated by an adverb "that" or "this."

Needless to say, the lack of articles in the Korean language both contributes to lack of precision, and presents enormous problems to Koreans (or Japanese) learning to use English articles.

Many teachers and parents reported that the child had the problem of omitting articles before nouns. For example, he would say, "This is book." He also had trouble knowing when to use an article and when not to. In some instances, this trouble came from not knowing if a noun is individual or collective noun. The child would say, "He bought a milk," instead of "He bought milk." He was also confused over which article, definite or indefinite, to use in a given sentence. He would say, "Yes, I brush a dog," instead of "Yes, I brush the dog."

Vocabularies

Vocabularies, as much as any other aspect of a language, reflect the values of a given society and culture. If a society puts strong emphasis on its kinship system and the maintenance of its strict hierarchy of social relationships, rather than the development of the individual, it tends to create vocabularies that would reflect and sustain those values.

In the Korean language, words describing kinship relationships are numerous and specific. The sister of father is referred as "*komo*," the sister of mother, as "*imo*," the wife of maternal uncle, as "*sukmo*," the maternal grandmother, as "*oe-halmŏni*," the paternal grandmother, as "*ch'in-halmŏni*," and so on. If there is more than one paternal aunt, the older one is referred as "*kun* (big) *komo*" and the younger one is "*chakun* (small) *komo*," and so on. Also, words denoting values relative to the maintenance of kinship relationships are numerous, such as duty, loyalty, filial piety, obedience, benevolence. These words are charged with emotion and meaning and used with frequency in daily verbal exchange.

On the other hand, those words that promote individualism and egalitarianism are markedly scarce. For example, there is no word for "privacy" or "preference." Words like "rights," "equality," "liberty," "justice," or "fairness" are used with less frequency. These English words do not have a great deal of meaning to most

Asians, largely because the concepts these English words represent have not evolved in Confucian tradition, but are borrowed from the Western culture. While these English words may excite positive feelings among Americans, they may likely to arouse negative feelings among many Koreans or Japanese. When these words were used with great frequency in Japan and Korea right after World War II, as Americans occupied the countries, a certain difficulty arose in translating them into the Korean or Japanese language. Although these languages have words that correspond to the denotation of these English words, their connotations are often markedly different, because Koreans or Japanese have different perceptions of these words. Their perception is influenced by their Confucian culture which does not have high regard for the concepts represented in these words. As a result, their meanings are often distorted to negative ones. For instance, in the minds of many Koreans, the word "liberty" is often perceived as "licence," or the word "individualism" equated with "selfishness" or "egotism." Anthropologist Clyde Kluokhohn writes in *Mirror for Man,* "I asked a Japanese with a fair knowledge of English to translate back from the Japanese that phrase in the new Japanese constitution that represents our 'life, liberty, and the pursuit of happiness.' He rendered, 'licence to commit lustful pleasure.' "[2] However, it should be noted that, as a result of increasing contacts with American culture and people, Koreans and Japanese today have a much better understanding and appreciation of these English words than they did 20 or 30 years ago.

The distortion of the meaning of these English words is closely related to the Confucian emphasis on the maintenance of the group and de-emphasis on the individual.

The de-emphasis on the individual often means the de-emphasis on the expressions of individual thoughts or feelings, which in turn does not give rise to new words, especially emotive words which are created by "the differentiated emotional and sensual experiences" of individuals. This is in part accountable for few Korean words that describe different qualities of emotions or things. Consequently, the small size of the vocabulary does not enable people to communicate with great subtlety and precision. Korenas tend to use adjectives, such as "good," "bad," "number-one," or "unperson" in a whole-sale fashion. For instance, the word "number-one" is frequently used to mean whatever is considered good or "on top." When in denouncing a person or his behavior, the word "bad" or "unperson" is often used, instead of a specific descriptive adjective. Needless to say, this tendency often results in an invidious description of a person's behavior, which in turn leads to misunderstanding or misrepresentation of the person.

Moreover, many Korean adjectives tend to have a quality of concreteness. This is largely because many of them are derived from Chinese characters which are based on the shape of an object or the relationship of persons. For instance, the word "kind" in Korean (also in Japanese) is made of two Chinese characters and pronounced as "*ch'in-jŏl*" in Korean ("*sin-setsu*" in Japanese). The character "*ch'in*" literally means "parent," while the character "*jŏl*" means "concern." So the adjective "kind" in Korean and Japanese is derived from the Chinese characters that literally mean "parent" and "concern."

7
Education

Despite many differences East Asians and Americans have in their cultural values and behavior, if there is one value they strongly share, it is education.[1] Generally speaking, all culture groups have their own share of highly motivated students, but certain groups tend to produce more of them than others. The clue often lies in a culture that provides motivational elements to achieve in education.

Strong Achievement Drive

In Korea, traditionally and today, the attainment of education is almost everyone's dream, because it is regarded as the ultimate key to the attainment of success and social status. This outlook has been handed down largely by the legacy of Confucianism. In old Korea, education was synonymous with a mastery of the Confucian classics and exegesis which defined the hierarchy of relationships, familial duties, and rules for propriety of conduct. In the legacy of Confucianism, as discussed in Chapter 3, "Social Structure," the worth of the individual is primarily determined by his sex, age or social status. Since sex and age are more or less fixed by birth, if a person wants to attain superiority above and beyond, one has to attain social status. In older times highest social status was attained by becoming a Confucian scholar. Only wealthy landlords could afford to educate their sons on Confucian ethics, because such an education required funds. At the end of his study, the student took a series of civil service examinations that tested his ability to repeat the text of the Confucian classics and exegesis in the most literal sense. If he passed the examinations, he was able to obtain a position in the bureaucracy. The rationale behind this system was that those who mastered Confucian ethics automatically became moral persons who had the ability to rule the people. Through his bureaucratic position, the scholar-bureaucrat exerted his political power as well as gained tributes from those he ruled. With money thus acquired he bought land and rented it to landless tenant farmers, collecting heavy levies of grain which he sold in the market. Thus scholarship on Confucian ethics eventually led to political and economic power.

Although today's education in Korea is not based on mastery of Confucian classics, much of its character, approaches and effects are inherited from the past. Education is still primarily a means to an end—the means to attain a degree rather than to train the mind. The ultimate goal of education today is to attain a Ph.D. degree, as it was to become a Confucian scholar in older times. This is why so many young people tirelessly pursue the attainment of their Ph.D. degree. Up to recent years, owing to Confucian tradition, literary education was greatly emphasized, while technical or scientific education was largely neglected. Even today, education, particularly beyond primary school, is a privilege bestowed to only a "special few," because it is supported by the student's parents and requires the passing of a series of entrance examinations. Only those who can afford the tuition and are bright enough to pass the entrance examinations can hope to go to a secondary school. Moreover, almost all parents try to send their children to highly-rated schools, often at great sacrifice, on the assumption that this guarantees better job opportunities after graduation, as well as enhances their social status. This is why a great many students aspire for entrance to highly-rated schools, and inevitably run into tough competition. Some students take exams year after year before they gain entrance. To prepare students for the entrance examinations, schools offer them extra classes after regular school work. In addition, affluent parents often hire tutors to help their children better prepare for the examinations.

As part of the preparation for such tough competition, parents instill in their child when very young the value of education. In the morning when the mother sends her child off to school, she exhorts him, "study hard" or "obey your teacher." When the child returns from school, the mother greets him, "Did you study hard?" When relatives, peers and teachers meet the child, they greet him, "Are you studying hard these days?" When they depart they say, "Study hard." Thus the child lives in a social milieu highly charged with innate respect for learning and the drive toward achievement in education. Not surprisingly, letters that adoptees received from their birth mothers or relatives were replete with such exhorting phrases as "study hard," "obey your parents," or "be a great person." One typical letter read: "Do things as you are told. You should be grateful to your adoptive parents. You owe them a great deal. Study hard and be a great person."

Such endless exhortations by his parents and others is bound to instill in a child the value of education and make him exert great will to excell in his study. Not surprisingly, the result of interviews with parents and teachers in the study shows more than 64% of the children (22) was rated high to above average in motivation, while 23% were to average and 13% were low. Many parents and teachers spoke of the children's strong achievement drive. A typical comment from parents was: "He is eager to learn and has a great will to do anything he puts his mind to." According to one father, when his teenage son ran away from home after a fight with him, he slept in the school yard of his junior high and went to school the next morning. Many teachers also described the behavior of the children as characteristically respectful and obedient, as well as highly motivated to learn. One teacher said, "Ann was respectful to me in every way. She always followed directions correctly and did what she was told." Another teacher said, "I wish more children were as eager to learn as Tom is. I wish I had a roomful like him. He is a delightful boy."

But one may ask: will the children's strong acheivement drive continue into the future? The answer will largely depend on the child himself, other factors in his American home, and the social and educational environments beyond.

Some Characteristics of Education

Primary school, for instance, lasts six years and is largely study- and discipline-oriented. Students go to school six days a week. A typical school day begins in the yard where all students assemble. Each class lines up in two rows with their teacher standing in front, facing them. At this time the school principal or teachers make announcements about daily activities or events. The whole student body engage in physical exercise (calisthenics); then march to their classrooms. As the students enter the school building they take off their shoes. At the end of each school day the students assume the responsibility of cleaning their own classroom, sweeping, cleaning and waxing the classroom floor and hallway. An average classroom has four or six rows of wooden desks; girls are usually seated on one side of the room and boys on the other. In the upper classes girls and boys do not usually share the same classroom.

In the Confucian scheme of relationships, the teacher is superior to the students by status, and assumes the authority to demand unquestioning obedience from them. His relationship with them is strict and formal, like that of father-son. Students address teachers by their family names plus "*sonsaengnim*"—a respectful term for teacher. In the classroom students are expected to be quiet and submissive to their teacher and follow his instructions without questioning. Most school hours are taken up with classroom studies. Students are given a heavy load of homework; if they neglect it or misbehave in school they are disciplined, often by corporal punishment. Such discipline is taken for granted, and parents as a rule make no recourse.

One 15-year-old adoptee, who came to the United States at age 11, did not like the Korean school system, but praised the American system. She said, "My Korean teacher had a long stick hanging by the blackboard. If we did something wrong, we were made to stand in the corner and had to lift a chair or desk above our head for a period of time. If we didn't get our homework done, we would get our hands whipped. If a student stole something, like a pencil or eraser, the teacher would make the whole class stand up and be searched, until someone confessed he took it. Occasionally the teacher would check our hands; if they were dirty, he would whip them. If our feet were dirty, we were made to clean them with our hands." In comparison, she said of her American teachers, "My American teachers are so nice. They talk to us as their friends and don't put us down. Teachers here have more patience and do not whip us. We don't get frightened by them, so we can ask them questions."

On the other hand, some adoptees who were accustomed to the strict, study-oriented system were disappointed with the American school system for its extreme permissiveness. One 19-year-old adoptee who came here at age 12 said, "I think the Korean school system is good, because it is strict and study-oriented. In school children are taught to behave and respect their teachers. Here in America, students don't respect their teachers as much. They talk back to them or laugh at them. I don't understand that. In Korea such a behavior was never allowed, even though you were right." Similarly, a 16-year-old girl said, "American teachers are just too easy—so I'm not learning as much as I did in Korea. Teachers in Korea are strict and wanted us to learn. That's all they wanted from us." The reaction of these adoptees to the American educational system is actually their reaction to the negative aspects of American public school system which is more permissive and less study-oriented than, say, American preparatory schools. Schools in Korea are more like American preparatory schools in many respects—more strict and study-oriented.

Today, as in the past, Korean students learn information or facts from text books, mostly by memory work. Students are tested mainly on their ability to memorize and reproduce what is in the text. One adoptive mother who adopted an 8-year-old girl said, "Diane has terrific memory powers in learning situations, but is usually terrible when it comes to remembering what mom said five minutes ago." Memory work is a learning method largely inherited from the Confucian past, when students were trained to memorize by rote the Confucian classics and tested on their ability to repeat as literally as possible what was in the text. Thus learning does not involve much exchanging and discussing ideas between teacher and students, evaluating the material they study, or producing a critical analysis, geared to develop their minds. Paul S. Crane writes in *Korean Patterns*, "Memory work is one of the main emphases in many Korean schools, and children are drilled excessively in such work. Because of this, Korean children are usually good at memorization and often surpass Western children of the same age in this ability. However, this is often at the expense of development of the ability to reason, to solve problems, to make evaluations, and to think originally or independently for oneself. This poses serious problems in life, especially in the scientific fields, for many students have never been trained to collect data, synthesize it, and come up with answers that are based on inductive reasoning."[2]

Memory-oriented education has many pitfalls. It often results in literal-mindedness and uniformity of thinking. While uniformity of thinking serves the government well in its efforts to control its subjects, literal-mindedness often makes communication between people extremely difficult and often results to misunderstanding. When students who have been educated on memory work are subjected to the American educational system, they may do well in studies that test memory ability but may have trouble in those areas which require the ability to reason or evaluate the material, because that requires an independent, creative mind. The following is a good example. A Korean student studying veterinary medicine at an American university failed an examination, and reportedly said to his professor, "If you had asked me questions which could be answered by reproducing what is in the text book, I could have answered all of them."

Traditionally, in primary school, there are few activities, such as the parties prevalent in American schools, geared to enable students to socialize. However, there are limited recreational activities. For instance, between the classes students go out in the yard to play. There are annual athletic meets, plays, music events and class excursions in the spring and fall. Class excursions are perhaps the highest point of all school recreations. Under supervision of teachers, the whole school goes on a day's excursion to famous historical sites or scenic places. One 15-year-old adoptee, who didn't like the punitive aspects of the Korean school system, recalled a school excursion. "The whole school goes on a picnic in the fall or spring to a park or scenic place. We see the greenery or the autumn colors. I really liked that part."

Preparing the Adoptee for American School

Many children arrive here from abroad with little schooling as well as little knowledge of English. For quite sometime they have no real verbal means of communication with their parents. To cope with this situation, many adoptive parents purchased English-Korean dictionaries and learned a few Korean words and phrases. For a while parents and child communicated in sign language as well as by using the dictionary. For instance, parents would read an English word in the dictionary and then let the child read its meaning in Korean.

When the child starts school, his language barrier can create many problems. One 18-year-old adoptee who came here at age 11 recalls his first few days in school. "I came on Friday and went to school on Monday. I was so scared. I didn't know a word of English. My tongue was tied. All the kids came to me and said, "Hi." I didn't know what they were saying; I thought they were making fun of me. So I got into a few fights." In Korea children normally do not greet one another in school, as American children do, with "Hi" or "How are you?" As a result, the adoptee, who didn't know a word of English or the American custom of greetings, naturally thought and acted the way he did. A little preparation for the child in terms of what he could expect in school could have saved him from fighting.

To make school less traumatic for the child, some kind of preparation is clearly needed before he is sent to school. One very thoughtful mother related how she had prepared her child before sending him to school, "About two weeks before school started, we invited Bob's teacher to our home so they could get acquainted in surroundings where he felt most comfortable. We were fortunate to have a patient, understanding teacher. She did a wonderful job of helping him adjust to school. She invited us to bring him to his classroom before school started, just so it wouldn't be so strange to him the first day. She also wrote and illustrated a beautiful little book telling how he came from Korea and how we adopted him. She shared this with the class and encouraged them to help Bob learn the things he needed to know. Later in the year, she invited me to speak to the class about Korea and bring Korean food for them to taste. Bob taught everyone to eat with chopsticks and the day was a great success."

In school English will be the most difficult subject for the child to master; he will need as much help from the parents as from the teachers. One mother said, "I worked with Bill almost every day after school for about half an hour. First he learned the alphabet, then consonant sounds, followed by vowel sounds and blends. We worked at his speed and gave much encouragement and praise for the smallest progress. We were fortunate to have an excellent teacher and speech therapist at school. With everyone working together, Bill began to understand the mechanics of the language. From this point his progress was more rapid. We then began using flash cards and playing word games. His reading is good today and improving. The main thing we're working on now is building confidence. When I think of all Bill has learned in the time he's been here I'm overwhelmed. We are so proud of him!"

In addition to parental assistance, most children received English tutorial assistance in school. Some parents provided the child with an additional tutorial assistance at their expense during the vacation periods. A majority of the teachers interviewed observed that while all children struggled with English, many of them excelled in math, art or athletics. At least they did far better in these areas than in English. Frequent comments from teachers were: "Math was his strongest subject. Language arts were his weakest subjects." One mother who adopted a 7-year-old boy said, "He is especially good at math, physical ed, music and art. Both his 1st and 2nd grade teachers feel he will be at the top of his class once his English is strongly established."

8
Family Dynamics

The Motivation to Adopt

To become parents of a child of another culture or race is a challenge, considering the psychological and cultural complexities involved in parenting such a child. As inter-country adoption became wide-spread and began to make newspaper headlines, the general public wondered why some couples would want to adopt a child from another country and culture. The overriding answer lay in the shortage of Caucasian babies available for adoption in the United States.

The majority of parents interviewed in this study contacted their adoption agencies primarily to adopt children of their own heritage, but learning that few Caucasian babies were available for adoption, they were persuaded to adopt a child of another country. The most often cited reasons for the adoption included the desire to create a family, to enlarge the size of the family, to balance the sex-ratio of the family or to provide a sibling to their other child, etc. These stated reasons were no doubt motivated by emotional needs such as the need to love and be loved, to help and be helped, or possibly to strengthen the bond between husband and wife through their common experience, or to project their own values or image onto the child, or to advance their career. While some of these reasons are clearly stated, others are not. However, one thing is certain: couples are motivated to adopt by a host of reasons, some of which are not always apparent. And there is no way to know fully how many forces are at work motivating families to adopt.

The largest group of couples in this study were childless for reasons of infertility, late marriage, lack of interest in giving birth to children, or being single. One mother who is a college professor said, "We were married late and didn't want to start a family. We applied at our agency to adopt a child, but learned there were no white children available for adoption. We were given an opportunity to adopt a child from Korea. Our only specification was age—we wanted an older child." Refreshingly, some couples in this group openly admitted self-interest as a prime force in their adoption but also expressed concern about displaced children needing homes. One mother who is firmly committed to a career outside the home said, "We decided not to have a biological child, but thought a child would add a special dimension to our lives. We recognize that we invested in the adoption for self-interest, but also out of responsibility for the children. Adoption is different in many respects. It takes more time, energy and effort to develop a relationship with the child. Because we have to work harder to earn and gain the child's respect and affection, it is a challenge for us."

One mother who was single at the time of adopting

her first child said, "I just like children and wanted to have a child who could be part of my life. It was sort of an investment for the future. There were few children available for adoption that I could find as easily as Korean-born children. There are a lot of children in the world that need homes. I want to help my children grow up to become good individuals. Also, I want to do fun things with them. But, I realize parenting is not all fun and games."

In this group a few couples adopted because their relatives or friends had adopted children from Korea. One father said, "My brother and his wife adopted Korean-born children. After seeing them doing well, we were encouraged and decided to adopt. Both of us were older when we married, and wanted to have a family at that point. Since my wife was working, we decided to adopt an older child who would fit into our life style."

The next largest group was composed of couples who already had a child or children of their own, but wanted their daughter or son to have a sibling of the same sex. One mother said, "Our plan was to have a boy and a girl. We had a boy first, then came our twin girls. The girls overwhelmed our son who had been getting all our attention. We thought it might be good to give him a brother. Then we read about intercountry adoption in the newspapers. This got us interested."

In some cases their first adoption led to a second, to give their adopted child a sibling of the same cultural heritage. One mother said, "My husband and I come from a large family. We love children. We had two boys and one girl born to us, and then adopted a girl. Then to give her a companion of the same heritage, we adopted a second girl."

The third largest group was made up of those couples who had only boys or girls and wanted the experience of parenting children of the other sex. Frequently these couples had two or three boys or girls born to them. If a couple had only girls, they chose to adopt a boy. If the couple had only boys, they chose to adopt a girl. One mother said, "We have three girls. We wanted to have the experience of parenting a boy, yet did not want to have any more children born to us. We felt we could accept and nurture a child from another race and culture, something we realize not everyone can do." Often one such adoption led to another. The same mother said, "After Bill became a part of our family we decided we wanted another. We felt it would be good to have two boys who could relate to each other in a special way."

Some couples in this group seemed to have been motivated to adopt a child to whom the husband or wife could be a role model or with whom they could share special interests. For example, the husband may wish to have a boy with whom he can play baseball or go fishing, or the wife may wish to have a girl with whom she may have a special mother-daughter relationship. Usually, when there was no girl in the family, the wife took the initiative to adopt a girl; and when there was no boy, the husband took the initiative. One mother said, "We hoped to have two children, a boy and girl. After our two daughters were born, my husband suggested we adopt a boy. As we explored the possibility, we found there would be a long wait for white children. But, when they showed us referrals of children with Korean or other minority backgrounds, one particular referral touched our hearts. His plight seemed enormous."

The fourth group was made up of couples who had children but were motivated by the need "to help the child." One mother said, "One day I read a story in a local newspaper about 'Amerasian' children who needed homes. I felt sympathy for them and wanted to do something for them. I feel I'm doing something worthwhile for my child. It may be a good selfish feeling."

A few parents adopted because of their interest in the culture from which the child came. A mother who adopted two children—a girl and a boy—said, "When we first decided to adopt a child of another race, we had thought of adopting one of Oriental heritage born in this country. We decided on an Oriental child because we admire Oriental people and their culture and because we felt such a child would be better accepted in our community than a black child."

Reaction from Relatives, Friends or Public

Initial reactions of close relatives to the family's decision to adopt were widely varied, ranging from enthusiastic to indifferent to openly critical.

Quite a few parents reported that their relatives for the most part approved or supported their decision to adopt. One mother said, "We have been fortunate in that most reactions from family, friends and strangers have been very positive." Another said, "We had no objections from our family—only my grandfather who is in his 80's had some reservations about black and asked if the child's skin color was light."

However, many parents experienced a mixture of reactions from their relatives. While some members of their families were supportive, others showed indifference or disapproval. After the arrival of the child, however, those who initially disapproved warmed up to him and accepted him as part of their family. A single mother who

adopted two children said, "My mother was very supportive from the very beginning. She really treasures the children. Even my aunt who initially didn't approve of the
idea is now raving about them."

Another mother of three daughters who adopted a
boy said, "My stepmother was enthusiastic, but my father
and my husband's mother were indifferent toward our
decision to adopt. Since the child arrived, however, they
have changed their attitude completely. Now he is their
favorite."

In face of negative attitudes, a small group of parents
processed their adoptions without discussing it with their
relatives. A mother of three children who adopted three
more said, "Our relatives would say, 'Don't you have
enough kids to take care of?' So when we adopted our
second child we didn't tell them." Some parents showed a
remarkable sense of independence and confidence that
they could make their own decisions concerning their
lives, regardless of the opinions of their relatives. One
mother of three children decided to adopt, despite the
opposition of her parents. She said, "Our parents balked
at the idea when we first mentioned it. They said, 'You
have enough children. What do you want another child
for?' But I could feel their objection was a smoke screen
for racial prejudice. Though our parents warmed up to
our son after his arrival, they always keep a cool distance
from him. This doesn't bother us as we can't change their
attitudes." One single mother said:

> When I found out it was possible for me to adopt, I
> started talking with friends and relatives. A lot of them
> said, "For a single woman to raise a child is a lot of
> responsibility." My father said, "It would burden you too
> much, it's too difficult for you." He had talked with a
> school superintendent who had known some people who

adopted Korean-born children and had problems. I was angry and said, "Just because some people have problems, it doesn't mean every child is going to be a difficult child to raise." My brother said, "Well, it will be a very difficult thing for you to do, but if it's something you want to do, go ahead and do it." Then I met and talked with some parents who adopted a child from abroad. They all had very positive things to say. Regardless of what others said, I was determined this was something I wanted to do.

In addition to the reactions of relatives, adoptive parents had to deal with that of their friends, neighbors and strangers. According to the majority of parents in this study, friends were usually curious and favorable, although some raised questions. Adoption changed some families' social life. A mother who adopted older children said, "When we decided to adopt our children, some of our friends called us 'nuts.' They asked, 'After all, why older children?' Now our friends are those who have also adopted Korean-born children. We have little time to see our previous friends who mostly have biological children."

Quite a few parents reported that some of their acquaintances made remarks intended to make them feel good, but which patronized the child. A mother who decided not to have a second "home-made" child said, "We often run into comments like this, 'How wonderful that you took two orphans!' Such a remark makes me angry because we adopted the children for personal reasons, not as a crusade to save the world!" Another mother said, "Many people will say they can't tell the boys apart. This reminds me of comments I've heard about Blacks: 'They all look alike.' I usually ignore these comments. The other remark we hear is how wonderful we are to have adopted these children and how fortunate they are. We look upon ourselves as the fortunate ones."

Some parents ran into various forms of unpleasant public reactions, such as unkind stares or open prejudice. Such experiences made them keenly aware of the existence of strong racism in the United States. One mother who adopted a half-black child with distinct negroid features said, "If I go to a grocery store alone, I have no trouble writing a check and cashing it. When Steve is with me, they always ask me to show them a driver's licence or identification. It's sort of their display of prejudice. They are saying in fact: 'If you're the mother of a biracial child, you're not quite as dependable, so we have to check your credit more carefully.' It angers me very much when I find that kind of prejudice."

Rewards

The kind of rewards parents claim to have had through their adoption may further clarify or give additional insights into their motivation to adopt.

Almost all couples interviewed in this study felt the experience of parenthood through adoption added a new dimension to their lives. This usually meant the opportunity to grow and change, as well as to give and receive love from the child. This especially seems to be the case for those who had become first-time parents by adoption. One mother who adopted two children said, "Our experience has been very positive and rewarding. So far it's great. It's delightful to have children, to hear about their adventures in school, to play games with them and to see them grow and mature."

Even those parents who have biological children seem to feel they have gained something from the adoption. One mother of three daughters said, "I feel we have been very fortunate to have had the experiences of parenting two little persons, who have become our sons in a different way than the children born to us. They have added a specialness to our lives. We have become a closer family because of the times we shared talking about their arrival, planning for that, then sharing, and working through the difficult and joyous moments. We feel we have been richly blessed by the addition of two little boys into our lives."

Adoption means not only rewards but trials and tribulations, especially during the initial months of adjustment. However, the majority of the parents seemed to feel the positive side far outweighs the negative. One mother of three children who adopted a boy said, "We see adoption as a challenge. When we are able to meet that challenge even on the smallest scale, we feel a sense of accomplishment."

For some families adoption was a learning experience which broadened the scope of their interest. They learned about and became more interested in the culture and the people from which the child came. One mother who adopted two older children said, "I learned a lot about Korea and its culture. On certain holidays the children would tell me what they do or did in Korea. When something about the political situation in Korea are reported in the news, they would tell me about the Korean war or about the Japanese rule over the country. I learned a lot of interesting things I didn't know before." Another mother who has two children said, "I feel we are privileged to be a part of another culture and life. We can look forward to experiences we would otherwise have missed, had we limited ourselves to our own immediate world and vicinity."

9
The Quest for Identity

All adoptees face a quest for identity. But for those adopted across racial and cultural lines, it looms larger, even more complex. No one can deny there is a great potential for serious identity problems for non-white children growing up in white American homes. Inevitably, at one stage or another, they are going to go through some degree of conflict about their identity. Such conflict often comes as they go through the stage of being "torn apart" by loyalty to their adoptive parents and their birth parents or as they strive to identify with their white parents while dealing with prejudice and discrimination in society because of their Oriental heritage.

How will they reconcile themselves to this dilemma? Some parents and professionals tend to believe the child needs to develop an identity inclusive of his ethnic heritage, and indicate their willingness to help him do so.

Often this help means giving the opportunity to learn about his ethnic culture, and letting him have some contact with children or adults of similar background or with his birth mother or relatives. But, since couples vary in their personalities and beliefs and in their ways of interpreting these questions, they do not completely agree on the answers. Can a child develop a healthy, personal identity within the framework of an adopted family of different ethnic heritage? How can such a child be exposed to his birth-culture or, more crucially, how can others of that same culture be approached and involved in his exposure? Finally, is ethnic identity really all that important in this "melting pot" society? Most parents try to deal with (or ignore) these questions in their own ways with varied results, depending on their beliefs, circumstances and the child's personality.

On the question of ethnic identity parents seem to be divided into two basic groups. One group does not see much value in the child's developing a sense of his ethnic identity. They feel it is better for him to establish stability in this culture, and that contact with other children of similar background or sustained interest in his former culture are thought to disrupt this process and often bring unwanted results. One mother who adopted older children said, "We found their contact with other children sometimes brought problems. For example, their comparison of material possessions often aroused feelings of jealousy and animosity in each other." A mother who came from Sweden said, "When I came here, I tried to remain Swedish and stayed so much with Swedish groups that I didn't learn about American culture. I now realize that was a mistake. I do feel it is more important the kids learn things American and acquire skills necessary and beneficial to their survival in the United States." Another mother who espouses the concept of a "melting pot" society said, "This is a mixed, free society. We should live accordingly, not emphasizing so much the racial and ethnic aspects. Our children want to become as American as we are and be accepted as such. They would like to live like other Americans and mix with people from all different backgrounds."

The other group of parents firmly believe a child needs to cultivate or retain some awareness of his ethnic culture and try to arrange opportunities for him to do so. They take him to Korean music concerts or art exhibitions, or encourage him to form friendships with other Korean-born children and adults in their community. Some invite Korean students and adults into their homes or attend Korean church services in their community. One mother who adopted a 7-year-old said, "Diane knows her mother is Korean, so she tends to identify with Koreans. We try to expose her to others of her culture, by taking her to Korean church services. She is enthusiastic about going to Korean church and meeting the people there. We have tried to acquire books in Korean for her, as we see some benefits in her being able to read Korean at least."

In addition, some parents corresponded with the birth relatives of the child. Such contacts usually began as the result of a letter from the birth mother brought by the child to his adoptive parents. One couple who adopted a 9-year-old boy received a letter from his birth mother saying, "I'm sad because I couldn't make him happy. I hope you will love him and make him happy as your real son always. I don't know how to thank you." The American couple answered the letter. This exchange was followed by more letters, along with pictures and gifts. The mother's letters to the child always contained exhortations like "study hard" and "obey your parents." The American mother said, "We are learning a lot as we try to help him feel pride and interest in both cultures. Some day we'd like to meet his mother. She raised him for nine years and we are raising him after that. We feel some kind of a bond between us." Another mother said, "Initially, I had some reservations about writing to the mother, but I answered the letter our child brought with her. After that we exchanged pictures, gifts, and more letters. I learned how she loved the child, what it meant to her to give her up, and how grateful she is to us for rearing her. All that changed my view of her. She is a beautiful person." It is apparent that these parents have developed positive feelings toward the birth mothers. Some experts believe this is a good thing, as these positive feelings can be passed on to the child.

While parents in this group made a conscious effort to give the child the opportunity to learn about his former culture and develop an interest in it, quite naturally they all hoped and wished their child would first identify with them and American culture. One mother who adopted two children said, "We wish both our children would grow up being proud of their Korean heritage. However, since they are to grow up and live in America, we want them to identify with us and the American culture, because this is necessary if they are to be well adjusted in this society."

On the other hand, quite a few parents reported that although they tried to help the child feel some interest in his former life or culture, the child did not respond to their effort. One mother who adopted a 8-year-old boy said, "When we inquired about the possibility of making contact with the birth mother, we were discouraged by the agency. He was happy that we sent some pictures of him to the mother through the agency, but, beyond this, he doesn't seem to have any desire to write her. He almost never talks about her or his experience in Korea. I would occasionally ask him, 'Did you do this with your mother?' He would say 'yes' or 'no' but did not seem to want to talk about it. Once on a bus ride, as soon as he saw some Asians, he made a point of looking away from them. It is obvious that he is trying very hard to forget about his past. Why wake the sleeping tiger?" Another mother who adopted a 6-year-old girl said, "After she arrived here, she completely rejected anything Korean. Once I sent her to a Korean dance class, but she hated every minute of it."

Rejection of their former life or culture is an inevitable course many children will take, because they have a lot of uneasy feelings (anger or shame) about the past. Many of them experienced deprivation and rejection or had disturbing relationships with adults. Yet, regardless of how they feel about their past, they have a fundamental need to understand and come to terms with what has happened to them and why they are where they are. Unless they have some understanding about this and are able to resolve their feelings, they will continue to live with uneasy memories, which are bound to interfere with their efforts to realize their potential. Clearly, these children may need additional help from their adoptive parents in understanding and meeting their needs, in order for them to feel secure about themselves. One mother who adopted a 7-year-old boy said, "When Jamie knew sufficient English, he told us how his father had left him alone in a big city and how the police took him to live in an orphanage with other children. He told us how his mother punished him once by putting him in a bag and tying it shut. It is difficult to know how much of what he tells about his past experiences is true or how much he has made up. He certainly doesn't seem to have many good feelings about his past and what he experienced. Thus he tends not to feel very okay about himself. He believes he can't do things as well as others. So we talk more about positive and negative feelings and tell him he is a beautiful person whom God loves and whom we have come to love. We try to reassure him that no matter how terrible he might act, we will never leave him. We try to make him see he is like a caterpillar in a cocoon who is emerging into a beautiful butterfly, capable of doing some neat things."

Whether or not the child has uneasy feelings about his past, the longer he lives with his American parents the more he is likely to identify with them and their culture. Some children even forget about the fact that they once lived in Korea or they look different from their parents. One 15-year-old girl said, "Since I live with American parents, I feel and talk like an American, but when I see myself in the mirror, I see a Korean face and get startled."

As part of the child's identification with his American family, it is also inevitable for him to feel some anxiety about his physical differences from his parents or others surrounding him. One mother said their 10-year-old boy strongly identifies with the family in all respects, but "He often looks himself in the mirror and seems concerned about his looks. I stress the beauty of human diversity." Another mother who adopted a 7-year-old girl said, "Jackie is very aware of her Oriental physical characteristics. When she saw herself on video-tape, she responded, 'I look Korean!' Her tone indicated she didn't want to look Oriental. I try to stress the positive aspects of her background." According to some parents, their children wished their complexions were fair or their hair were blond like their parents or friends.

Furthermore, there are reasons to believe that the child's identification with her American family and culture is often expedited by the antithetical differences in the cultural orientations and values in the two countries. Once a child learns to identify with American culture, he finds it difficult to identify with Confucian culture. Language is a good example. If the child lived with his American family and spoke English everyday, it would be difficult for him to retain his past language, because the languages are in many aspects antithetical. Almost all parents reported that in the few months their child had been with them, he had completely forgotten Korean. The younger the child the faster this process occurs.

However, sooner or later, these children will face a dilemma, as they grow up and venture out into a society which is often hostile to racial minorities and will discriminate against them or subject them to derision. A popular assumption is that their parents would not be able to sympathize or help them effectively cope with these situations, because they themselves have not been subjected to similar discriminations or derision. One can well ask, "How can they teach their Oriental child the 'survival skills' needed in a racist society, when they have never needed to develop such skills themselves?" This reasoning is strongly reflected in the objections of black social workers to white couples adopting black children.[1]

Almost all children in this study encountered incidents of racial slurs or name-calling, hostile or not, directed at them by their peers or strangers. They were called a variety of names—"Chinese" or "chink" or "Jap" or even "nigger" or other racial epithets, such as "flat nose" or "flat face."

How to deal with such racial slurs is a serious problem facing these children. Cited in the following are some representative examples of name-calling incidents children encountered in school or playgrounds, and how their teachers and parents dealt with the situations. Some ways are clearly more effective than others.

Teachers' Handling of the Name-calling Incidents

- A boy called Amy a nigger. I explained to the boy what the name meant and told him it was not nice to call names and asked how he would like to be called names.

- Betty did have trouble on the bus with name-calling. These were children from outside her classroom. Her classmates were protective and fascinated by her. They were mortified to hear kids making fun of her. We tried to find the kids and talk to them individually. I also talked to Betty about having darker hair, etc. and told her that children probably will remark just like they do about children who are very blond, fatter or skinnier than usual, or who have speech problems.

- Name-calling did not happen or was not allowed in my classroom. When Jimmi was not present, I talked to the other children about him belonging to our school family—and told a little about his background. I asked their help and they all responded beautifully. I also wrote and illustrated a book "Why is Jimmi smiling?" One of the closing statements said. "Because you are his friends. . . ." I'm sure there were instances on the playground or bus that I was unaware of. On one occasion I heard a child from another room call him a "Jap." I made it a point to talk to this child about it and to my knowledge he did not repeat the offense.

Parents' Handling of the Name-calling Incidents.

- Our two girls were called "Chinese" in school. I explained to them that they didn't know the difference between Chinese and Korean and said "Don't let it bother you."

- Boys at school called them "Chinks" or "Chinese." They were baffled and did not respond to them. Not responding or ignoring is the best solution.

- Kids at school called John, "Chinese Eyes," and he was upset by it. I told him, "Be proud of your eyes. Don't let it bother you."

- In school one boy came over said, "How come you have a flat nose and slant eyes?" I suggested to her that if this happens again, she should tell the person, "I have lived in two countries. How many countries have you lived in?"

- Both boys have had instances of name-calling in school and out. The boys get called "Chinese" a lot and get mad because they are not Chinese.

- John and Mary were called "Chinese" at school. Mary was also called "flat nose." I discussed this problem with my sister-in-law, who is Oriental and had similar experience as a child. It was her recommendation that I encourage the children to ignore the name callers. However, this does not mean we ignored the situation. I spoke with both children's teachers about this and both classes had special programs about differences and likeness in people, presented in a positive manner. I also visited both classes, bringing Korean foods and culture items. This was accepted enthusiastically. Unfortunately, Mary was not able to ignore the name calling directed at her. She is a very sensitive child and was very upset. It took much love and understanding for us all to get through this. We helped Mary overcome her anxiety about this by sympathizing with her, and giving her extra love and security. I bought the book "Chinese Eyes" and read it to her and John. I also told them the story of how God made people different just as he made the flowers different, so the world would be a prettier place.

As in the incidents just described, many parents advised their children simply to ignore the name-caller or explained that the name-callers did not know the difference between Chinese and other Asians. Though ignoring the name-caller might avoid an immediate confrontation, it does not resolve the child's confusion or hurt feelings. If at some point he does not defend himself, the effects of such insults will be insidiously destructive to his mental health. Therefore, parents and teachers have an urgent responsibility to confront the name-callers in the child's behalf, as well as to help the adoptee understand the meaning of prejudice and racism. Otherwise the insults will be repeated and the child will continue to suffer psychic injury.

Name-calling is a projection of hostility onto a group different from one's own. Psychiatrists often view racial slurs as a defense mechanism used against another racial group by someone who is usually insecure or unhappy with himself. That is, if a person feels good and secure about himself, he doesn't have to put someone else down. Joyce Ladner writes in *Mixed Families* about racial slurs black children (adopted by white couples) had been subjected to: "One has to raise serious doubts as to whether these, or any other children can go through life simply ignoring the verbal insults and discrimination they encounter. At some point, the average child can be expected to exercise some kind of defensive tactics in his or her behalf."[2]

While recognizing the problems of racial discrimination existing in the United States, a majority of the parents tend to emphasize individual identity above all. One mother defined identity as "a composite of ancestry, education, ability, intelligence, how you feel about yourself, how others see you, things you plan to do in the future. Of these, I believe how you feel about yourself is the most important." Another mother went even further in her emphasis on individual identity, by minimizing the importance of ethnic identity. She said, "Identity means to me inner-self, that is, what a person feels. What I'm most concerned about is what I am or what I want to be rather than who I am. I don't think nationality is important." Many adoptees also tended to stress individual identity more than any other. One 18-year-old boy who came here at age 11 said, "The nationality aspect isn't that important. I want people to think of me first as an individual who has a certain kind of background."

The American emphasis on individual identity is a unique aspect of American culture which clearly separates it from Confucian culture. It is a byproduct of American ideals which value the individual and his spiritual being far more than his sociological attributes. Firmly dedicated to this ideal, many parents feel that if they accept a child as a unique individual and love him as such, the child will develop a sense of his individual worth and, thereby, a strong, healthy identity. They, like many experts, believe that having a loving and accepting parent is the most important thing for a child's well-being, and that if the child has a strong, emotional link with his parents, he can cope with most of his problems in life with minimum difficulty.

Notes

Introduction

1. Helen Miller, "Recent Development in Korean Services for Children," *Children*, vol. 18, no. 1 (Jan.-Feb. 1971), pp. 29-30.
2. Today intercountry adoption is rapidly expanding its horizons around the world—particularly, India, Colombia, and other Latin American countries.
3. Abram Kardiner, *The Psychological Frontier's Society*, (New York: Columbia University Press, 1945), p. 414.

Chapter 1: Physical Adjustments

1. Edward and Margaret Norbeck, "Child Training in A Japanese Fishing Community, ed. Douglas G. Haring, *Personal Character and Cultural Milieu* (Syracuse, New York: Syracuse University Press, 1968), p. 658. According to the authors, infants in the Japanese fishing community were also given foods like rice gruel, clear soup, grated apple etc.
2. *Kimbap* (*sushi* in Japan) is equivalent to the American sandwich.
3. Ruth Benedict, *Patterns of Culture* (Boston: Houghton Mifflin Co., 1959), pp. 2-3.

Chapter 2: Emotional Adjustments

1. Claudia Jewett, *Adopting the Older Child* (Cambridge, Mass.: Harvard Common Press, 1978), p. 251.
2. Jacqueline McCoy, "Identity As a Factor in the Adoptive Placement of the Older Child," *Child Welfare*, vol. 40, no. 7 (September 1961), p. 15.
3. Marjorie Margolies, *They Came to Stay* (New York: Coward, McCann & Georghegan, 1976), p. 156.
4. Ibid., pp. 319-320.
5. Edward and Margaret Norbeck, "Child Training in A Japanese Community," ed. Douglas G. Haring, *Personal Character and Cultural Milieu* (Syracuse, New York: Syracuse University Press, 1968), p. 656.
6. Jan de Hartog, *The Children* (New York: Atheneum, 1969), p. 138.
7. Ibid., pp. 57-58.

Chapter 3: Social Structure

1. Edward Norbeck, *Changing Japan* (New York: Holt, Rinehart and Winston, 1965), p. 70.

Chapter 4: Methods of Discipline

1. Ruth Benedict has noted that Japanese mothers also use this method to stop the crying child, in *The Chrysanthemum and the Sword* (Boston: Houghton Mifflin Co., 1946), p. 262.

Chapter 5: Personality

1. Ralph Linton's Introduction to Abram Kardiner's *Psychological Frontier's Society* (New York: Columbia University Press, 1945), p. viii.
2. Ibid., p. xii.
3. L. Takeo Doi, "Giri-Ninjo: An Interpretation," in *Aspects of Social Change in Modern Japan*, ed. R. P. Dore (Princeton, N.J.: Princeton University Press, 1967), p. 327.

Chapter 6: Language

1. The word order of Korean and Japanese sentence structure is exactly the same; also, both languages are similar in other aspects, as discussed in this chapter, largely owing to their common Confucian heritage. Their major difference is their native phonetic systems.
2. Clyde Kluckhohn, *Mirror for Man* (New York: Wittlesey House, 1949), p. 154.

Chapter 7: Education

1. I use the term "they" here in a qualified sense, by referring to a majority of social and economic classes in Korea and mainly the white middle-class in the United States.
2. Paul S. Crane, *Korean Patterns*, 3rd ed., (Seoul: Kukje Publishers, 1974), p. 40.

Chapter 9: The Quest for Identity

1. Joyce A. Ladner, *Mixed Families* (Garden City, New York: Anchor Press/Doubleday, 1977), pp. 80-81.
2. Ibid., pp. 251-252.

Bibliography

Adams, John E., and Kim, Hyung Bok. "A Fresh Look at Intercountry Adoption." *Children*, vol. 18, no. 6, Nov.-Dec. 1971.

Anderson, David. *Children of Special Value*. New York: St. Martin's Press, 1971.

Benedict, Ruth. *The Chrysanthemum and Sword*. Boston: Houghton Mifflin Co., 1949.

————. *Patterns of Culture*. With new preface by Margaret Mead. Boston: Houghton Mifflin Co., 1959.

Brooten, Gary. "The Multiracial Family." New York *Times Magazines*, 26 September 1971.

Buck, Pearl S. *Children for Adoption*. New York: Random House, 1964.

————. "I Am The Better Woman for Having My Two Black Children." *Today's Health*, vol. 50, no. 1, January 1972.

Caudil, William A. *Effects of Social & Cultural Systems in Reaction to Stress*. New York: Social Science Research Council, 1958.

———— and Devos, George. "Achievement, Culture and Personality: The Case of Japanese Americans." *American Anthropologist* 58: 1102-1126.

Chang, G. S. C. "A Cursory Comparison Between Chinese and English on Precision." *Elementary English* 49, March 1972.

Chang, Tung-Sun. "A Chinese Philosopher's Theory of Knowledge." *Etc.* IX, Spring 1952.

Chin, Robert and Ai-li. *Psychological Research Communist China*. Cambridge, Mass.: MIT Press, 1969.

Cohen, Lucy M. and Fernandez. "Ethnic Identity and Psychocultural Adaptation of Spanish-Speaking Families." *Child Welfare*, vol. 53, no. 7, July 1974.

Crane, Paul S. *Korean Patterns*. 3rd ed. Seoul: Kukje Publishers, 1974.

Creel, H. G. *Confucius and the Chinese Way*. New York: Harper & Row, 1960.

Curtin, Katie. *Women in China*. New York: Pathfinder Press, 1975.

Daniels, Michael J., S.J. *Through a Rain Spattered Window*. Seoul: Taewon Publishing Co., 1973.

Diamond, Norma. *K'un Shen: A Taiwan Village.* New York: Holt, Rinehart and Winston, Inc., 1969.

Doi, L. Takeo. *The Anatomy of Dependence.* Translated by John Bester. Tokyo: Kodansha International Ltd., 1973.

———. "Giri-Ninjo: An Interpretation." In *Aspects of Social Change in Modern Japan,* edited by R. P. Dore. Princeton, N.J.: Princeton University Press, 1967.

Donoghue, John D. "An Eta Community in Japan: The Social Persistence of Outcaste Groups." *American Anthropologist* 59: 1000-1017.

Earle, R. A. and Wong, A. Y. T. "Cultural Constraints in Teaching Chinese Students to Read English." *The Reading Teacher* 25, April 1972.

Embree, John. *Suye Mura.* Chicago: The University of Chicago, 1964.

Fraiberg, Selma H. *The Magic Years.* New York: Charles Scribner's Sons, 1959.

Fromm, Erich. *Psychoanalysis and Religion.* New Haven, Conn.: Yale University Press, 1971.

———. *Escape from Freedom.* New York: Rinehart and Co., 1941.

FitzGerald, Frances. *Fire in the Lake.* Boston: Atlantic, Little, Brown and Co., 1972.

Halloran, Richard. *Japan: Images and Realities.* New York: Alfred A. Knopf, 1969.

de Hartog, Jan. *The Children.* New York: Atheneum, 1969.

Hochfeld, Eugenie. "Problems of Intercountry Adoptions." *Children,* vol. 1, July-August 1954.

Herbert, Jean. *An Introduction to Asia.* New York: Oxford University Press, 1965.

Hsu, Francis L. K. *Americans & Chinese: Reflection on Two Cultures and Their People.* New York: Doubleday & Co., 1971.

Ishino, Iwao. "The *Oyabun-Kobun*: A Japanese Ritual Kinship Institution." *American Anthropologist* 55: 695-707.

Jewett, Claudia L. *Adopting the Older Child.* Cambridge, Mass.: Harvard Common Press, 1978.

Kardiner, Abram. *The Psychological Frontiers of Society,* New York: Columbia University Press, 1945.

Kim, H. Edward. "Seoul: Korean Showcase." *National Geographic,* December 1979.

Klibanoff, Susan and Elton. *Let's Talk About Adoption.* Boston: Little, Brown & Co., 1973.

Kluckhohn, Clyde. *Mirror for Man.* New York: Whittlesey House, 1949.

Kluckhohn, Florence, "Dominant and Variant Value Orientation." In *Personality in Nature, Society, and Culture*, edited by Clyde Kluckhohn and H. A. Murray. New York: Alfred A. Knopf, 1953.

Kirk, H. David. *Shared Fate*. Montreal, Quebec, Canada: Glencoe Free Press, 1964.

Ladner, Joyce A. *Mixed Families: Adopting Across Racial Boundaries*. Garden City, New York: Anchor Press/Doubleday, 1977.

Lebra, Takie Sugiyama. *Japanese Patterns of Behavior*. Honolulu: University of Hawaii, 1976.

Lee, Dorothy D. *Freedom & Culture*. Englewood Cliffs, N.J.: Prentice-Hall, 1959.

Levenson, Joseph R. *Modern China and Its Confucian Past*. Garden City, New York: Doubleday Anchor, 1964.

Levi-Strauss, Claude. *Structural Anthropology*. Translated by Claire Jacobson and Brooke Grundfest Schoepf. New York: Basic Books, 1963.

Lifton, Betty Jean. "Orphans in Limbo." *Saturday Review*, 1 May 1976.

———. "The Cruel Legacy: The Children Our GIs Left Behind in Asia." *Saturday Review*, 29 November 1976.

Loescher, Gil, with Ann Dull Loescher. *The Chinese Way*. New York: Harcourt Brace Jovanovic's, 1974.

Lyman, Stanford M. "Japanese-American Generation Gap." *Society*, January-February 1973.

Malcolm, Andrew H. "South Korea Seeks to End Flow of Orphans to Families Abroad." *New York Times*, 8 August 1977.

Mathews, Linda. "Despite Popularity, Cute Korean Babies Aren't for Export." *Wall Street Journal*, 7 January 1977.

Margolies, Marjorie and Gruber, Ruth. *They Came to Stay*. New York: Coward, McCann and Georghegan, 1976.

Martin, Samuel E. "Speech Levels in Japan and Korea." In *Language in Culture and Society*, edited by Dell Hymes. New York: Harper and Row, 1964.

McCoy, Jacqueline. "Identity As a Factor in the Adoptive Placement of the Older Child." *Child Welfare*, vol. 40, September 1961.

Miller, Helen. "Recent Developments in Korean Services for Children." *Children*, vol. 18, no. 1, Jan.-Feb. 1971.

Minami, Hiroshi. *Psychology of the Japanese People*. Toronto, Canada: University of Toronto Press, 1971.

Moloney, James Clark, M.C. *The Magic Cloak*. Wakefield, Mass.: The Montrose Press, 1949.

———. *Understanding the Japanese Mind*. New York: Greenwood Press, 1968.

Moore, Barrington Jr. *Social Origins of Dictatorship and Democracy: Lord and Peasant in the Making of the Modern World.* Boston: Beacon Press, 1966.

Nakane, Chie. *Japanese Society.* Berkeley and Los Angeles: University of California Press, 1970.

Norbeck, Edward. *Changing Japan.* New York: Holt, Rinehart and Winston, 1965.

―――― and DeVos, Georg. "Culture and Personality: The Japanese." In *Psychological Anthropology*, edited by Francis L.K. Hsu. Cambridge, Mass.: Schenkman Publishing Co.

―――― and Margaret. "Child Training in A Japanese Fishing Community." In *Personal Character & Cultural Milieu*, edited by Douglas G. Haring. Syracuse, New York: Syracuse University Press, 1968.

Parson, Talcott. *The Protestant Ethic and the Spirit of Capitalism.* New York: Charles Scribner's Sons, 1958.

Pye, Lucian W. *The Spirit of Chinese Politics: A Psycho-cultural Study of the Authority Crisis in Political Development.* Cambridge, Mass.: MIT Press, 1968.

Rathbun, Constance, and Kolodny, Ralph I. "A Groupwork Approach in Cross-Cultural Adoptions." *Children*, vol. 14, no. 3, May-June 1967.

Rondel, Florence and Murray, Ann-Marie. *New Dimensions in Adoption.* New York: Crown Publishers, Inc., 1974.

Sidel, Ruth. *Women and Child Care in China: A Firsthand Report.* New York: Hill and Wang, 1972.

Smith, Warren. *Confucianism in Modern Japan: A Study of Conservatism.* Tokyo: Hokuseido Press, 1959.

Solberg, F. E. *The Land and People of Korea.* New York and Philadelphia: J. B. Lippincott Co., edition 1973.

Texter, Robert B. *Failure in Japan: with Keystones for a Positive Policy.* New York: The John Day Co., 1951.

Trumbull, Robert. "Amerasians." New York *Times Magazine*, 30 April 1967.

Weber, Max. *The Sociology of Religion.* Translated by Ephraim Fishoff. Boston: Beacon Press, 1964.

Whiting, Beatrice B. and John W. M. *Children of Six Cultures: A Psycho-cultural Analysis.* Cambridge, Mass.: Harvard University Press, 1975.

Whorf, B. L. *Language, Thought, and Reality.* Edited by John B. Carroll. Cambridge, Mass.: MIT Press, 1956.

Wong, Jade Snow. *Fifth Chinese Daughter.* New York: Harper and Row, 1945.

Wright, Arthur. *Confucianism in Action.* Stanford, Calif.: Stanford University Press, 1959.

Index

Since the mid-1950's, more than 30,000 Asian children have been adopted by American families. Many of these children were old enough to have absorbed much of the Confucian culture of their homelands; many brought culturally acquired behaviors with them. Since cultural differences between East Asia and America are enormous, the families involved necessarily made many adjustments. But little has been written about the cross-cultural experiences of these families.

Frances Koh, a former adoption worker, knows intimately both the American and Confucian cultures in which she has lived. *Oriental Children in American Homes* is the result of her bicultural experiences, her extensive research on psychological anthropology and cross-cultural adoption, as well as her interview with over sixty couples, their children and teachers. She describes fundamental differences between Confucian and American cultures in a wide range of areas such as language, food,